A Perfect Day

Guide to a Better Life

Joseph E. Koob II

ISBN: 0-9665218-0-3

Cover Designed by

Jennifer Elbert

FIRST EDITION

Dedication

I dedicate this book to all the people in my life who have made it possible--all of those people who been instrumental in helping me learn what is enclosed herein. Most especially in recent years to: Lisa, Carol, Barb, Stacy, John, Jana and my two wonderful children Elise and Nathan.

Special thanks to the people who helped with the many drafts: Tammy, Jennifer, Lisa, and Phil

Joseph E. Koob

NEJS Publications

Lawton, OK

Contents

8

Introduction

❦

Have you ever wanted to have a perfect day? **The** "Perfect Day." A day when everything and everyone seems to fall into the right places in your life, and you could not wish for anything else. A day when, as the old commercial used to suggest, you could truly say at the end, "It doesn't get any better than this!" A day when from the moment you wake up, until you finally, almost reluctantly lay back down to sleep you were, alive, happy, content, peaceful! A day of joy and bliss that you can carry with you for the rest of your life?

Is such a day possible?

Bill Murray, as "Phil" in the movie **Groundhog Day**, discovers that by some quirk of fate or curse he is forced to relive the same day over and over again. Caught in this seemingly endless repetition of a truly lousy day in his life, Phil wonders why he couldn't have another day of his life repeated over and over--a day perhaps like the one where he met a girl on the beach and they made passionate love all day long. However, through many thousands of repeated days, Phil finds himself discovering an unusual, hidden truth about life--that his "bad day" is his to make over and over and over, until he gets it right.

Or perhaps it is not so much that Phil get the day right but that he makes the effort, that he has the power, to make the day whatever he wants to make it. To make it his "perfect day." He makes the choices. He makes the day.

Do you ever wonder if perhaps that is why we are here; to find our own version of the perfect day. Perhaps we don't get the chance like Phil does to *re-do* a day ad infinitum until we get it right. But if you really think about it, is one day so much different from another that we can't learn from it and the next and the next so that with every "repetition" it gets better--we get better--closer to our "perfect day."

This book is about working** toward our own personal perfect day. From the time you get up in the morning until you go to bed you will discover the choices you make that make your day--for better or for worse. And ultimately, I hope, we will see (you and I--because I am still working also) that the perfect day is there for us. We just have to make it happen and then make it happen again and again and again.

So perhaps this book is mostly just a way

10

for you to realize this fact--to put your life into a perspective that each day presents for you exactly what you need at that time and you realize it and thank God for it. But you also can realize that each day is a process that you are the focus of, that you happen to be the one person who has the power to direct and change what this day **means for you**.

Perhaps the most difficult thing for us to really realize is that every day **is** a Perfect Day--we just have to accept that fact. The day you just had was a perfect day, because of all the things you have done and learned, all the people you have been involved with, all the ways you have gone along your path in life. Until we can fully understand this, we have work to do. That's what this book is really for--working toward an acceptance of your complete physical and spiritual self in this universe.

And suddenly you and I, I hope, will know that this day and all of those days in the past and those to come in the future is, have been, will be perfect days.

Work: Unfortunately, the word work tends to have negative connotations in our society, but the word play does not quite fit here either. I will use this word a great deal, and for the purposes of this book I will be referring to the positive effort you are making for yourself toward having a perfect day. I look at this effort as something I look forward to every day. It probably **is more play, than work for me, but as you will find out, even though this can be pleasurabl, it is not always easy. So the concept of "hard work" does apply. I'm pretty confident, though, that you will enjoy a lot of this "work."

Preface

❦

Okay, let's face it, we're all different. No one is going to approach life exactly the same way as someone else, so you need to consider this entire book as a collection of suggestions. Some will fit you and some won't. Take the ones you can use; disregard those that you can't and be sure to make up your own as you read along. Remember this is your perfect day, not mine. If it helps--I'm out there working on mine, too. Maybe we all are; it's just that some of us don't know it yet.

This book attempts to emphasize two contrasting perspectives: the joy of freedom and creativity contrasted with the consistency and control of establishing positive habits for yourself. It will challenge those of you who are free-spirited and creative in one direction and challenge those who tend to be more controlled and orderly in your lives in another. Experiment with both, you'll find that, depending on your tendencies, some things will be easier than others. Above all else, have fun and do what is best for you.

There will be many ideas thrown out here.

Some I have discovered on my own through trial and error, many I have learned along the pathway of life from friends, relatives, acquaintances, even strangers. And even others I have found in books and tapes from many, many people including well-known self-help "gurus." I will try to recognize and share with you and often recommend as this work progresses.

Also, it's not a contest. If you beat me to the perfect day, or beat your neighbor, spouse, boss--That's great! But you haven't won anything and you probably won't get to the perfect day if it's a contest against yourself or someone else. Even though everyone you come in contact with in this effort will benefit, you're doing this for yourself. So be selfish about this work. The prize is your day and the many, hopefully, perfect days that will follow. My hope is that you're having such a perfect day that you don't even know it, and it just melds into the next perfect day. That is my wish for you and for myself.

Remember, too, that if you are having a perfect day or even just working toward a perfect day, that your influence on all life around you will be more positive. The ripples from your personal striving can...no, **will**, have a profound effect.

I hope to make this book a totally positive approach. Many self-help books tell you what to do AND what not to do. I'm going to try to stay away from the "**don'ts**" as much as possible. I think that by suggesting what you can do that there is already the implication of what not to do. We have spent most of our lives being told what not to do. It's time to focus on what we can do and even better yet, having the power to select from not only many positive suggestions, but from our own creativity as well. So enjoy doing!...for yourself and others. And when the "don'ts" arise in your life, find a way to re-categorize them into do's.

Happy work lies ahead!

Guidelines

❦

These are some general ideas to help you throughout your work. You will see them again and again in the specific suggestions detailed in the main body of the text. If you get discouraged come back to these few pages and remind yourself that the fundamentals are pretty basic, but we often get lost in the details. Many of these just seem to grow out of each other.

It's easy and hard to have a perfect day! But I think you will find that as you work on this--most of the time, the work will get easier--like falling into a groove.

Find the grooves you like and continue with them; change whenever you feel the urge. Go with **your** flow.

Love!

Why? It's a great feeling! I feel good when I am loving. I feel better about me, the world, everything. What a great emotion to have--just think what your life would be like if you could surround your days with love...impart that feeling to others...pass it around...have it come back to you. Wow!

Read on. It gets even better than this.

love yourself!

Above all else **love yourself!** Paramount to the process is being a kind, loving person **to you**. Encourage yourself, support yourself, and always take time for yourself. In order to have a perfect day you need to enjoy it--you need to enjoy being you. You will probably be reminded often of this very important perspective.

Many people have given this advice to us in many ways, but I like Robert Heinlein's direct approach in his novel **Time Enough for Love**: "If you don't like yourself, you *can't* like other people." If you don't like who you are, then you need to work toward accepting yourself or changing those things you don't like.

BUT--even more importantly--remind yourself of all the amazing things about yourself that you can and do like. After all, you, yes, **YOU**, are an amazing person. You have survived all kinds of trials and tribulations to date, you have accomplished a tremendous number of things in your life, and you're on a wonderfully positive path because you wouldn't be reading this book otherwise. Love yourself for all those things and love yourself for moving ahead.

love others

Loving others is, I truly believe, an extension of loving yourself. You won't find many religions or philosophies that don't espouse this basic rule and after all it makes sense. I think and feel that if we truly look into ourselves that we are at the root loving creatures.

You can go by the Golden Rule or any other predicate, but the basic meaning is the same. Find time every day to specifically practice this "Rule." At some point, I hope you and I will reach a level where we are able to love all those people we come in contact with and all those people we influence throughout our lives.

[I would encourage you to extend your love to other creatures as well.]

19

Be kind!

Being kind to yourself and others is just another extension of the whole "love thing." What is especially important about this, though, is it is that something more specific that we can work on throughout our day.

Wayne Dyer, this comes from several of his tapes (see the Bibliography at the end of the book), adjures us with "Whenever you have a choice between being right and being kind. Be kind." It feels good to be kind to others. It often brightens their day and in the whole process you start brightening your own day. What a great way to live!

Be honest!

❦

Be honest with yourself and others. Remember good ol' Shakespeare? "To thine own self be true, And it shall follow, as the night the day, Thou canst not then be false to any man." This is another one of those biggies that we find in the Bible and lots of other places.

This opens up a whole series of questions-- like who you really are, what you really want in life, what are the really important things, and so on. We won't answer those now, but we'll probably get back to this one fairly frequently, too.

Ponder this for a few minutes: If you're not happy, what is it that is making you unhappy? I can almost guarantee it's something inside yourself reacting to something outside. Get to the root and make some changes inside if that's what's called for, and the outside part won't matter so much--if at all!

Being honest with yourself might seem painfully hard at first, but you'll be really surprised at how it opens your eyes and changes your life.

Have fun!

❦

Have fun! Enjoy yourself! Having fun is part of the process, too. Whether you are working, dealing with people, exercising, driving down the road, or even resting/meditating you should be enjoying what you are doing. If you're not, find out why and adjust.

Ask yourself why you aren't enjoying where you are at that specific moment in time and that specific place. You might be surprised at some of your answers, and how asking that question changes your perspective so that you look for ways to enjoy yourself even in the most mundane of tasks.

This might even have some bearing on the previous guideline of being honest with yourself.

Humor!

Humor is different from fun. Fun should be all the time--enjoy your life. Having fun with life--adding humor to your life and others is a way to relax and look at things just a little bit differently. The reason we like comedians like Bill Cosby, Seinfeld, George Carlin, etc. is because they are willing to look at just about anything to do with life in a humorous way. If you start getting into ruts this is a great way to get out of them.

P.S. You'll have more fun!

Be creative!

Be creative! Creativity is the spice of life. If you can think; you can be creative. Explore the possibilities of your day by opening up yourself to new ways of looking at things and new ways of doing things: approaching people, problems, work, everything! You'll have more fun and you'll like what you find out about yourself and the extraordinary imagination you do have. The more you use it the easier it will get.

Try being creative in the strangest places and times. Why do we always put the same sock on first? Why do we always drive the same way to work? Why do we always mow the lawn one way? You'll be surprised at what you can come up with and you'll have a whole lot more fun, too.

Use this book!

What I mean is: write in the margins, underline, scribble, cross-out, add your own thoughts--take the book with you and wear it out. Copy passages you want to remember and tape them to your refrigerator, your walls, your forehead. Share them with others as that might help you with your path, too, and what you share with them might just be something wonderful for their day, too. If you are having a good time with this book, share it with others because you care about them and their having a perfect day.

Wear it out.

Take notes!

❦

Take notes **for yourself**! This is not an exercise for a test. Writing things down can help you remember them and then you will have important ideas readily available that will help you toward your perfect day.

What I mean is that you should jot down things that you want to remember. Thus you will have them available at specific points in your day. Write the ideas in a small notebook or on 3 X 5 cards or even an electronic notebook. Carry them with you in your car, purse, wallet, or even put them on your wall or in your desk. Laminate them if you think they're going to get a lot of use. Eventually you will be able to remind yourself as you get "into the habit" of doing some of these things, but this is very useful to start with.

Learn! Learn! Learn!

❧

Don't forget to **learn!** This IS worth repeating three times! Since life is a process of learning, you will grow toward your perfect day. It may take awhile. It took "Phil" thousands of Groundhog days. You don't have to become a great pianist, the best basketball player, or the top executive in your firm. You have to be the best you for you. You need to find out what is important and right for you. If you exercise every day, then find what goal is right for you for that moment and go for it. Tomorrow will bring other challenges and goals.

Always keep in mind that the ultimate goal in this challenge is to have your perfect day--not someone else's--your's. You need to decide what that means for you and what you need to do to get there. Use the book; use your wits; use your own creativity.

Cultivate your garden!

"Cultivating your garden" might just be construed as a synonym for learning, but I believe, as I think Voltaire believed, that this is more than that. It is a nurturing of yourself in which you learn as part of the process of nurturing.

If you nurture your **self** I truly believe you will also nurture those around you and the world. Try it. You might be surprised at how good it feels.

This might be one of the most difficult parts of this whole process because you need to find out exactly what this means for you and it's hard for me to make specific recommendations about how to nurture your self, your being. However, I think you will enjoy cultivating yourself and the world and people you come in contact with.

Make time for yourself!

❣

Have time for yourself, often. Many books and gurus recommend meditation. We will come to that, but for now spend your **self-time** any way you like. Find a few minutes at various points in the day to spend by yourself, with your **self**. This can mean quiet contemplation, meditation, a walk through a park, five minutes sitting with your eyes closed in your favorite chair, a short nap, a brief period of remembering someone you cherish, or a thousand-thousand other possibilities.

This is rejuvenation time! Find out what works for you. Try different things and use the ones that work best. This really is enjoyment time--every day!

Share yourself!

❦

This is an active growing you are undertaking. It involves considerable contact with all those unique people you come into contact with everyday. **Sharing yourself** with them is part of having a perfect day.

Whether it is a smile or kind word to a stranger behind a counter, a friendly greeting to an acquaintance, or intimate contact with a significant person in your life, these are all important parts of your day--every day. I think you will find that every person you meet will become part of your perfect day. That's why they're there.

communicate!

Sometimes--often--you may think you are being open, honest, and clear about who you are and what you are trying to say, but the other person really just doesn't understand. Good communications, that arrive at true understanding, take effort. If you have ever been an educator you know this intimately. You have to try lots of different things sometimes to get the point across. And it is often very surprising at what ends up working.

Sometimes it takes an effort on your part to make sure you are understood AND to make sure you are understanding the other person--because communication implies this is working both ways. By being honest and kind and through creative effort you can improve your ability to communicate tremendously.

$\mathcal{P}_{ay}\, \mathcal{A}ttention$

❦

I don't mean to me--I mean to yourself and the world around you.

Interestingly, I added this to the guidelines after writing nearly the entire book--It just kept popping up throughout the text. One of the reasons we don't make the most of our lives is because we just forget to pay attention. When you pay attention to the birds, the flowers, your spouse, work, the sensations of living, life itself, and the world, you suddenly are more alive--more "in-tune" with what **life** is all about.

Try to spend some time each day making the effort to pay attention to what you are doing, who you are with, where you are, what you are feeling, and how you are reacting. You will notice that you are having more fun, feeling more energized, and enjoying life more. Other people will notice, too!

Try paying more attention to others, too. They will really appreciate it and you will learn a great deal about life in the process!

Listen!...

❦

to yourself...

The hard part about this is listening to yourself. When we **pay attention** to what we actually say in the course of a day we can discover a great deal about ourselves. AND we can begin to adjust our own speech to reflect a more positive outlook to everyone.

and others...

Everyone appreciates someone who takes the time to listen and who makes the effort to understand what is important to them. Cultivate good listening habits; consciously make an effort every day to pay attention to someone else's viewpoint. You will likely learn something about life, you will learn something about them, and you will learn something about yourself.

Be Patient!

✾

While I have listened to many self-help tapes, read many books on many subjects dealing with self-improvement both directly and indirectly, and meditated on all of these, I still have much to learn and process:

Be patient with your learning and growth process. We learn by doing and experiencing, and it does take time.

Be more than patient with yourself. It will pay off. Go back to your sources of inspiration--**often**--whether it is this book and/or other books, tapes, people, meditation, or just a nice place to sit and enjoy. Notice the things that do go well and when they don't, find the time and space to rejuvenate so that your process can continue. Especially when you notice yourself being particularly hard hit by frustrations, depression, trials and tribulations, things that you don't understand or don't seem to fit into your picture of life as it should be. That is when it is most important to step back, be patient, be kind to yourself, love and nurture yourself, support yourself, share yourself.

You will then be patient and kind with others, too!

Yeah, but....

🍒

Every recommendation in this book can be answered with a "Yeah, but...." "Yeah, buts," are not acceptable when it comes to your life.

Hey, this is so important I'm going to say it again:

"Yeah, buts," are not acceptable when it comes to your life.

And again:

"Yeah, buts," are not acceptable when it comes to **YOUR life**.

"Yeah, buts," are excuses. Do you want the answer for your life to be an excuse? When you meet God, whomever or whatever you believe God to be, do you want to answer the questions about your life with "Yeah, but I...."

I think that would make me just the teensyest, weensyest bit nervous!

Whenever you come up with a "Yeah, but...," or any other excuse for that matter while reading this book , I urge you to go back to the guidelines listed above, and especially the "Eleven Recommendations for a Better Life" (see just below), and then ask yourself how your excuse fits into these guidelines.

Ask yourself if you are just copping out. Ask yourself how your "Yeah, buts..." are preventing you from moving ahead with your "Perfect Day" work. Ask yourself if there are ways to begin to overcome the excuses that are preventing you from enjoying your life.

Find a close friend to practice "yeah, buts..." with: i.e. share your ideas/dreams and then "yeah, but..." them. Then let your friend brainstorm with you why these "Yeah, buts..." are unacceptable. Reverse your roles. You'll be surprised at how this helps your thinking and helps create new ways to look at things and new ways around the old "Yeah, buts..." in your life.

Just one quick example: There are NO excuses, NO "Yeah, buts...." for **"Love thyself and others."** There just aren't.

Think about it!

Synthesis/Analysis/Synthesis

❧

This is a complex way of saying look at the forest sometimes and not just the trees. It comes from a great educator I had the good fortune to study with at the University of Illinois--Dr. Charles Leonhard. We often tend to spend a great deal of our time in life taking things apart to understand them better, and this certainly has its place, but keeping a perspective of how it all fits into the big scheme of things is also very important.

Our analysis of the world and everything in it IS important to our understanding of life. However, try to spend a part of each day stepping back and looking at the whole (**synthesis**), no matter how much dissecting you have done in the meantime (**analysis**). And always, before you start dissecting/analyzing something take a look at how it fits into everything else (**synthesis**). It will give you a perspective to start from and a perspective to come back to.

Spirituality

❦

I believe we are spiritual beings. I believe there is more to our selves than this physical body. I am not here to espouse a particular religious faith or set of beliefs. I truly feel that the focus of this book and its recommendations for pursuing the best possible physical and spiritual life for yourself are in harmony with all religions and faiths.

Your own spiritual awareness and beliefs are very important to help guide you in working with any of the suggestions in this book. Follow your true spiritual self and you will not, cannot, fail.

Have more fun!

Check yourself often--are you having **fun**, yet?

If this is just work, you're not going to get there. A perfect day is not, should not, be hard labor--just striving for perfection in your life. While that may seem to be contradictory this "work" is a labor of love--for yourself and for others. If you're not enjoying this process, you need to step back and re-evaluate.

"Eleven recommendations for a better life."

Or Things You Can Do to Make Your Life Better

LOVE   THYSELF AND OTHERS

BE KIND (to thyself and others)

BE HONEST (with thyself and others)

HAVE FUN

BE CREATIVE

LEARN

CULTIVATE THY GARDEN

MAKE TIME FOR THYSELF

SHARE THYSELF WITH OTHERS

PAY ATTENTION/LISTEN (to thyself and others)

BE PATIENT (with thyself and others)

How to Read This Book

❦

Any way you like!

But! Let me make a couple of recommendations:

If you can, read this book in small pieces and get your "work" started really well after reading one section. This will give you a marked advantage because you will be able to focus your attention, make some significant changes to a small part of your day, get yourself off to a great start, and give yourself a boost in confidence about your ability to really persevere.

Another plan could be to read the book all the way through and then go back and start working from the beginning in small pieces. Do whichever one works best for you. However, you are the true judge of what you are capable of, so chop off what you feel you can handle.

If you decide to start from the "**BEGINNING**" (see immediately below) and work your way through the book, since the book is set up chronologically you will be starting the night before your "Perfect Day" and working through an entire 24-hour day.

I think you will also find that as you work on one section and slowly build into other sections of the book, that you will experience a tremendous amount of growth that will help make subsequent sections easier to approach. You'll find that there are many similarities between sections of this book in regards to problems and recommendations. You'll also find that everything eventually ties into the "Guidelines" above, so keep coming back to them anytime you have a question. You will find the answers you seek there--it just may take some soul-searching.

Beginning

How do you start this process? My first suggestion is **to start the night before**: This is not some elaborate plan you have to make, simply a thoughtful processing of a few ideas, perhaps a little planning, and most importantly a commitment to start the process (or continue it).

Remember, however, that any suggestion I make is up for your creative revision, so handle this "stage" any way you like; any way that is right and comfortable for you. If you are the kind of person who likes to have things detailed and organized, by all means make as detailed a plan as you wish. Just remember that nobody out there will know about your plan, and therefore you always have to be ready to revise if things don't happen the way you have them laid out.

Make a commitment to start the process

This is the most important thing you can do for yourself and it is something you should do each night before each new day of your work toward your perfect day(s).

Why is this so important?

Because once you take this step you are putting yourself into a mode that brings your awareness toward yourself and your growth-- toward your truly enjoying life. You will therefore spend at least some of the next day thinking about how to make that day better for yourself. I can't think of a better way to start getting the most out of life.

In a sense you will be watching yourself and how you react--interact-- deal with the world. Through a very simple commitment you will become more aware of who you are and how you relate to everything and everyone around you. It's like waking up from a foggy sleep. Try it once. I think you'll be surprised at how much energy this seems to give you and how much more interesting the next day of your life is.

You'll also have to get into this "habit"

by reminding yourself each day until it becomes second nature. You'll find that at the very end of this book I lead you right back here.

Don't forget!

Think about what a perfect day means to you

Take a little time, perhaps five minutes, to think about what a perfect day would be like for you. Do this every evening, before your next day.

Now, generally speaking we're talking about tomorrow--not some hypothetical perfect day on the beach in a tropical paradise--but if that is a goal you would like to attain some day, put it on your list for future perfect days (we'll address this more later on). Right now I'd like you to concentrate on having as perfect a day as possible **tomorrow**.

That may seem like an insurmountable task at this moment in time. You probably can immediately come up with a thousand reasons why tomorrow can't possibly be a perfect day for you. Remember, however, that we have to start someplace and this is your starting point and we want to be positive, always, so we're going to concentrate for a few minutes every evening on what you can do to have the best possible day tomorrow.

Concentrate on the positive things you can do--if you want check the **_"Eleven recommendations for a better life."_)** and/or the whole section under *Guidelines*. If you have certain things you want to focus on, then spend a few minutes thinking about how you might implement them. In addition, if you have underlined or noted specific items from this book or other books, make some mental notes on how you might be able to work those into your day.

Keep it short. After all, you're probably a little (a lot?) tired. You can always add things in subsequent days. You might want to just take one item and focus on it for a few minutes.

I'm not going to tell you how to go about this. You can sit in a chair and meditate on it, lie in your bed just before you fall asleep, or do it while you brush your teeth. Whatever works for you. I do think it is important, though, to be able to focus on these positive thoughts for a few minutes, so whatever that means for you...whatever it takes...

When you have paid the next day some attention, smile to yourself and get some rest. Tomorrow's already a better day!

Go to Bed with a Smile

❧

Take at least one minute to pat yourself on the back for the day just past. It may not have been your perfect day. It may have even been one of those not-so-good days. But I bet you did some really great things, and I bet you made a lot more progress than you might be giving yourself credit for. Remember love yourself; be kind to yourself; be really honest with yourself. It pays great dividends.

As you get more and more into this book, you will see that patting yourself on the back will be pretty easy, because you really have been working hard on all kinds of important things (like the **Eleven Recommendations...**). Just think about some of the successes you've had!

Find a pleasant thought to go to sleep with. It can be part of your plan. It can be just something or someone you love, something pleasant you remember, or just a special thought for that moment. Try to keep that thought, idea, image with you as you drift off. Smile. You'll remember it in the morning. You might even wake up with a smile. Pleasant dreams.

Getting Started

❦

Bang! You're awake. It doesn't really matter how--whether it's your alarm, your "sixth sense," or the dog barking next door--you're conscious and it's time to get started. So what do you do first?

I recommend staying right where you're at (in bed?) and at the very least take the time to remember the commitment you made the night before. This is just you reminding yourself that this **IS** your day.

Your Day

❦

This **IS your** day. It may be your first stab at a perfect day or your ten thousandth. It's still yours and you can do what you want within the parameters of what this day is set up to be in your life.

Okay, here we need to divert just a little bit from your wake-up call for a minute. As mentioned earlier this is probably not your fantasy day. That day on the beach or whatever tweeks your fancy might be in the cards, but you'll need to plan for that, and what we want to accomplish here is to make this "every day" day a perfect day. This might be just a "normal" workday for you, or a "normal" weekend day, or it could be some different or special day. You could be going on vacation, have a party that night, have a big evaluation at work, or even face spending this day in some not-so-pleasant-to-be situation e.g. at your mother-in-law's. (Why do we always pick on the mothers-in-law?).

Whatever it is, we want to make it the best day possible. So all the suggestions that follow can be applied to any kind of day. Remember--get creative if the suggestion doesn't seem to directly apply to your situation or this specific day you are about to face.

Take some extra time

Yup, you're right. You should do the planning for this the night before, but this is where it applies and hopefully you read far enough ahead to have gotten this into your planning. This goes directly to one of the ***"Eleven recommendations for a better life."*** "Make time for thyself."

Wayne Dyer (see Recommended Readings) recommends that you get up between the hours of 3 and 6 AM as this is a great and peaceful time to just be. And he's right, I've tried it; I've gone on 3 AM walks and runs and it is a wonderful time to be with the universe. However, you may not be up for 3 AM wakeups and 3 hour walks. So if you're not there are other possibilities for you. Read on....

Richard Carlson in ***Don't Sweat the Small Stuff...and it's all small stuff*** suggests that you get up an hour or two early and have that time to and for yourself to accomplish things before your kids, wife, etc. grab your attention or just to have some quiet time for yourself. And he's right, too.

But, I'm going to play it really conservative here and suggest that you start small and when it's right for you to do the 3 AM thing, do it. Or when you want to expand the getting up earlier for more quality time with yourself, do that. I recommend that you get up five, ten, maybe fifteen minutes earlier than normal and use that time for preparing for this day, getting in touch with yourself, just plain enjoying the quiet and peace.

Morning people/Night people

I think most of us recognize that there are morning people and night people. The morning people may already get up earlier than everyone else, and the night people don't want to have anything to do with getting up any earlier than they have to. So to the morning people I say, use your extra time in the morning wisely, as much as possible within some of the parameters/suggestions listed below, and to the night people I urge you to use your extra night time in this pursuit, but to also make that effort to have at least five minutes or so in the morning where you can have this bit of peace with yourself and the universe.

Using Your Extra Time

❦

You're committed to the extra time. How do you use it?

Lie there in bed, or sit on the edge of the bed and start your day as you ended the previous one. Think of pleasant things. Remind yourself of this day you are going to have and the positive things you're going to do to make it your day. Keep focusing on the positive. If you have trouble letting your mind slip into habits of worrying about something that lies ahead, or all the work you have to do, all those nagging things in your head, then just try to focus on something pleasant: a pleasant memory, a person you like, a moment in time, a beautiful scene. Do this for as long as you are comfortable. Initially you might only make 30 seconds or one minute. That's fine. You'll probably find you enjoy this little bit of time so much that you will eventually extend it.

Love someone

There is one important thing that I think would benefit all of us every day. This is a suggestion from Richard Carlson (***Don't Sweat...***) and I like it so much I hope he doesn't mind my adding it here with some embellishment. Before you dive into the day, think of someone to love.

This may seem redundant when you consider "Love thyself and others," and we want to love everyone, but this is someone (or someones) you pick out every morning to **specially** focus love to. It can be your significant other, someone you knew in the past, a relative, a friend, even an enemy, or someone you just feel needs some extra special love for this day. Just decide who it is and think of them with loving, happy thoughts.

This little item takes very little time-- perhaps a minute or two and it reaps so many benefits you will be amazed. First of all it puts you into a positive, loving mood right from the get-go. You will very likely remember that feeling and that person at odd intervals during the rest of the day, and then you can send those loving thoughts out anew.

Its really not important whether you believe that these loving thoughts will actually help that person, but they will help you, your mood, your feelings, and hence the mood and feelings of others you come in contact with. And just think, IF your loving thoughts do somehow filter through the universe and help that person, WOW! You've done something wonderful, and positive, and special and it only took a minute or two of your time.

I started doing this about three months ago, and at first it was pretty intermittent because I would forget (all of those other things we THINK are important tended to occupy my early morning thoughts far too often), but I kept at it and now I almost always remember. Sometimes I don't remember right away and it might pop into my head while shaving or dressing, but some time before I actually get to work, I remember, and I take that moment, right then, to think of someone and go with those good, loving feelings. Sometimes it is the first person who pops into my head; sometimes it is a person I choose because I really do love them in a special way and I want them to know it; and sometimes it's just someone I select for a wide variety of reasons. Sometimes it is even myself--especially if I am facing a day that bodes being more difficult than others. (Yes, we all have those.)

It is nice sending yourself love. Try it!

Get things done

Of course, this depends a great deal on how much extra time you have allowed yourself, but you have many choices about using "your time." Here are a few. I recommend you brainstorm many others, especially those that really work for you. You probably won't be able to or even want to do all of these every morning. You might want to alternate or just settle on one. These recommendations are also viable throughout the day or in the evening.

Meditate

Spend five, ten, or more minutes lying in bed, sitting in your favorite chair, or in some comfortable position and relax. Allow yourself to go deep within and find your inner peace.

I am now in the habit of doing at least a brief morning meditation. It usually includes my choice of who to send that special love to for the day and maybe just some peaceful, loving thoughts. Or it may include a prayer to help direct me through a concern or problem. Whatever you choose you will find this a great way to start the day:

Diversion One: Meditating

❦

You'll find that there are as many ways to meditate as there are people recommending that you meditate. They are all correct--because meditation is a personal issue and it has amazing benefits. The main purpose is to get to a place within yourself where you are at peace.

It is not a trance-state or something that reflects any particular religious orientation. You are allowing your inner self to come to the surface, while quieting the "noisy" side of your mind. You want to get away from the nagging, worrying part of your being and focus on all that is within you that is peaceful and loving. If you are troubled by the term "meditation" use the word "prayer." I believe prayer, for many people, is a form of meditation.

You can do this in a wide variety of ways. Some types of meditation involve mantras and chanting (like repeating ah-h-h, oh-h-h, om-m-m, or something else in your mind or out loud); other people use pre-recorded tapes to help them focus and subsequently quiet the busyness in their minds; and still others focus on a series of steps to help them become relaxed and peaceful. I have used a variety of techniques, almost all involved with visualization, imaging, and relaxing deep breaths.

Here are some ideas: Take some deep breathes in through your nose and release them slowly through your mouth, while focusing on relaxing your whole body. Use whatever imagery helps you to relax all the muscles in your body and in particular tension areas (imaging waves of relaxation flowing through your body work well).

Imagery

The use of imagery in meditation and a variety of other techniques in this book is a very useful skill to develop. (For example, I used imagery through meditation just recently to see myself recovering quickly from major sinus surgery and having little bleeding and swelling. I didn't bleed hardly at all from after the first day and had very little swelling!) Imagery is simply the ability to see what you want in your "mind's eye." Meditation helps you focus on that imagery.

You can take any of the *"Eleven recommendations for a better life"* and make some goals for yourself. Take "Love thyself and others"--create an image of what that means to you and its importance and you **will** work toward it. Use meditation to help focus your imagery and will.

Meditation imagery

Continue your meditation using a wide variety of imagery. For instance, imagine you are standing at the top of a set of 20 stairs. Focus enough so that you can see the stairs and the railing and then slowly descend focusing on each step and reminding yourself to relax more and more with each step. When you get to the bottom you should be very relaxed and peaceful.

If intruding thoughts and worries interfere with this process, start over or try again another time or another day. Meditation is a technique that you learn through practice. You are relaxing yourself and focusing your mind inwardly.

At the point where you reach the bottom step, if you have stayed relaxed and focused on what you are doing, you are already meditating. Let your mind wander peacefully or focus on whatever images help you stay relaxed and peaceful. I like looking at a blank screen--or the blue sky--where I can "write" things that I want to focus on. Mostly I use words like

"love," "peace," "harmony," "health," etc. I
even write them slowly on the screen in golden
letters. Some people find focusing on a
beautiful white (or other colored) light is a
very positive meditative experience.

If you want your meditation to be less
directed, then once you are in a relaxed and
peaceful state just let your mind take you where
it may. Sometimes this "non-control" can be a
little scary, but you'll find it very
invigorating and sometimes amazing ideas and
images pop into your consciousness.

By all means start meditating with help
from a tape or suggested sequence if you wish,
and then build whatever works best for you.

Special Places

I have my own "special place" that I often
go to when I meditate which is derived partially
from a childhood memory and partially just my
active imagination: a small lake up against a
beautiful mountainside and a log cabin where
inside I find my favorite lounge chair. By
walking down through the tall grasses to the
lake and cabin I relax and finally end up
sitting in my wonderfully comfortable stuffed

chair. Often I vary the "scenery" a great deal--adding a rainbow I can dance in (I even sometimes catch and "drink" the colors in a beautiful chalice), or animals I can greet on the way, etc.

Rejuvenate!

Once you have developed meditative and imagery techniques, meditating is one of those things that you can do for yourself every day at any time during the day where you can find time to relax. (If you get good at relaxing, even five minutes can be enough and very invigorating.) Ideally you can spend fifteen to thirty minutes or even more meditating, but use the time you are comfortable with sparing at that time of the day. Right after you get up may not be the ideal time for you; you might find evenings work better. And it's okay if you ultimately fall asleep (unless you have an appointment, in which case set an inner--or real--alarm clock) as that may be exactly what your body/sub-conscious needs.

Imagine yourself on a raft floating down the river...or sitting comfortably on a wonderful pile of pillows under a shady tree....or on the beach...whatever is the most pleasant, relaxful place you can imagine being.

Be patient with yourself--meditation takes practice--focusing inwardly takes practice. Start with very short relaxations or meditations (2-5 minutes) and build up. Sometimes the short meditations can be quite revitalizing.

Why?

People also view meditation in a wide variety of ways: access to the inner world or spirit; access to the sub-conscious; prayer, to find peace; a way to practice and reinforce affirmations (Short sayings that you wish to affirm for yourself or within yourself, like "I am a healthy and loving being."); or just a simple way to rejuvenate during the day. Use it anyway you like and think of it in whatever sense works for you.

I believe that if you do meditate that you will find yourself more at peace with the world (and much less stressed!), have more energy, and enjoy life more. Try it a few times and see if you can find your niche with this process.

This is one of the recommendations of this book that you will want to keep reminding yourself to do until it becomes a habit. It is that good for you!

Using Your Extra Time (cont.)

❦

Do something for yourself

You know all of those things you've always wanted to do and didn't have the time: this is the time. And if you think that the extra ten, fifteen, twenty minutes or so that you set aside in the morning isn't enough time, multiply it by thousands of days--that's the rest of your life, hopefully!

So get off your duff and start it--whatever "it" is.

This can be that novel you always wanted to write or read; something you wanted to build or make for yourself, your kids, your spouse, or some mornings it could just be a few odd little tasks that are so much easier when there is peace in the house, and you don't feel like you have to rush to get there.

Whatever you choose, **remember that this is a peaceful time,** and if you start putting pressures on yourself you will lose sight of the whole point. If you only get a half page of that novel written or one piece of board nailed into place, or one small task completed--you have done something that you hadn't done before and you should feel good about the progress and think pleasantly of what lies ahead in continuing this work (play?).

This is what I like to think of as "doing-time" or sometimes as "puttering" time (see "Vacations and weekends near the end of this book for an extension of this idea). If pressure (self-pressure/time pressure) enters the picture, I just stop and try something else or get on with my day. Keep it peaceful, relaxed, and focus on pleasant thoughts about what you are doing.

Take a walk/run/bike ride

There are two primary ways I perceive this particular recommendation: one is as exercise (which we will talk about later and is certainly a legitimate way this time can be used), the other is as one would look at a peaceful walk in which you commune with nature, the universe, God, or whatever you want to focus on.

I think there is a distinct difference for me between exercising for keeping in shape, building muscles, flexibility, etc. and doing an exercise activity just to be outdoors and with nature. Even though I exercise regularly for fitness, the times I have gotten up at three in the morning and taken long walks or runs have been more of a peaceful time outside with myself and whatever nature and the world offers me. Yes, I got a fair amount of exercise, but that was not the focus.

The image I have in mind for this (short or long) activity is again focused on being peaceful with oneself at a quiet time of the day: taking a walk outside and listening to the early morning sounds, breathing in the fresh air, and just genuinely enjoying life. This can take five minutes, or however long you have set aside.

Getting Ready for Your Day

❦

Doing the everyday "tasks" of getting ready for your day may seem like a ho-hum, endless repetition of mundane chores: going to the bathroom, shaving (face, armpits, legs, etc.?), showering, deodorant, make-up, contacts, and more. However, there are several things that have already made this day less ho-hum than perhaps before.

One thing is you are on a mission for yourself, you are directed and you probably already have just a bit more zip than usual.

Another is that you have spent at least a small amount of time thinking pleasant and loving thoughts. The world already looks better so lets keep it going.

But before we get into the "Getting Ready" phase of your day, let's take our first major diversion. I'm going to stick these in every once in a while just to be a little unpredictable (creative) and to cover some really important points that don't necessarily fit into any single place during the day.

Diversion Two: Exercise

❧

Some people like to exercise; some don't. Even if we want or like to exercise most of us don't get enough of it, especially if we have settled into a "desk job." I'm one of those people who likes to exercise, but I don't always have the time or energy to do so, and my job does not have very much built in exercising.

First of all let's talk a little about the importance of exercising. You may eventually decide it's not for you, so as with all of the things in this book this will be one recommendation of many you can choose from.

You've certainly heard about the benefits of exercise from a health standpoint, so I won't belabor that point.

More to the point of this book is that exercise does help you to feel better--both in the short and long runs. Short term gains from exercising are in an increase in alertness and energy ("just clearing out the cobwebs") ; long term gains come from being in better physical condition and thus feeling better overall, potential to lose weight if that is a concern of yours, and generally **a better self image.**

Self-image

And it is the self-image part that really strikes home in reference to this book.

Try this brief exercise: stand in front of a full-length or near full-length mirror nude....yup, in your all-togetherness. Appraise what you see--be honest with yourself. If you don't like what you see, what can you change and what will it take to change it?

Again you will have to make an appraisal based on what is realistic and what might be long-term fantasy. For instance: there's not much that exercise can do for your nose if you want it changed--so a long term goal might be to save enough money for a nose job (or any other part that can't be adjusted by exercise).

You can decide that you want to: lose ten, twenty, thirty or more pounds, tighten up those abs, or whatever. Try to get a picture in your mind about how you want your body to look. Keep that image with you and **you will** work towards it.

I can't over-emphasize the importance in almost any thing you try to accomplish or any recommendation you try from this book of gaining a perspective, an **image** if you will (see **imagery** above), of what you want the end result to be. This effort puts a picture in your mind of your ultimate goal(s), and that picture is all important toward getting to the end result.

You make the choices

Those of you who are reading this book are all different: different shapes, ages, physical abilities. And these unique characteristics may be tempered by many other factors including injuries, handicaps, etc. **If** you decide exercise is something you want to pursue, do it realistically **with the primary goal of adding to your existence in some fundamental way**.

Start slowly and build toward whatever image/goal is important. I hope you find that the important thing here is that you are finding pleasure in what you can do with your body. You will become aware of the many good feelings and extra energy that come from working with this wonderful machine that we have.

The goal or image you are pursuing, though important in setting the tone for exercise, eventually **becomes secondary to the significance of your being more in tune with your physical self and the physical universe.** After all, unless it is of little consequence to your own personal growth, our physical presence in the universe is a part of our existence.

I sort of look at it from the standpoint that God gave me this wonderful body to live in and I want to take as good a care of it as I can while I'm in it.

And it feels good to do so, too.

So what can you do?

There are thousands of possibilities. From the short walks mentioned above in regards to your early morning time to serious physical conditioning.

Do what feels good. This is very, very important.

Start out with things you enjoy. Expand your time/exercise if you want to.

You can get involved in team sports, or just do something for yourself. [I used to play basketball until I kept getting injured and then I decided God was trying to tell me something, so I started running instead.] If you like variety, try different things and alternate. Adjust what you do by any factor that affects yourself and your enjoyment of the activity: weather, location, amount of time you have, etc.

Some days you may literally have to push yourself out the door, even though you planned ahead, the time is there, and you have already started your exercise program. Make a decision for yourself, however, I will offer one piece of advice: it is very rare that I don't enjoy exercising and get a great deal from it once I do get out the door. It might even take me a mile or so to get "into" those better feelings. So if you can, try getting over those small (large?) bumps in the road that might discourage you from even starting. You'll probably find it was worth it.

Some specific suggestions

get help

A very important point: if you are start-ing an exercise program it is a good idea to check with a health-care professional concerning what you have in mind and any considerations or restrictions you should consider. It's also valuable to work with or talk to a fitness expert or guru for specific recommendations.

get up and move!

This is a good recommendation for all of us with desk jobs. As an administrator I tend to spend large blocks of time at my desk. However, I have recently made it a point to try to get up off my duff' at least once every hour and walk somewhere: to say hi to my employees, to physically mail a letter rather than hand it to my secretary, to just get up and walk outside and smell the fresh air. It's amazing how much this rejuvenates oneself. **It is** exercise, and it can really add up over the weeks and months and years--those thousands of days you have left!

set a regular time

If you find it useful, **set a regular time** to exercise. I actually change my "regular time" fairly regularly, particularly as the seasons change: I typically run outside in the mornings during the summer, in the afternoons in the spring and fall, and exercise inside lifting weights, stationary bike-riding, running in the winter.

start slow and build

Be patient: this is yours to control. Find what works. If it does work, and you find you are benefitting **and enjoying** what you are doing--expand. Remember *Have Fun*!

remind yourself

Remind yourself--often! The way I do this is through redundancy. I keep a dumbbell in my bathroom (and sometimes set myself a goal to do some "lifties" every time I enter the bathroom), another dumbbell in my office, my treadmill is in my bedroom (at least for the moment), and the riding bike and other weights are in the garage. If I get busy and don't make it out for my run, I usually end up doing at least a little something, somewhere.

get creative!

Do whatever it takes to make this fun for yourself. My treadmill and bike are in front of TV's, and I move my tape/CD player (boombox) wherever I need it when I am exercising indoors and even outdoors when I lift weights or practice Taekwondo. Then I can listen to self-help tapes, music, or whatever. I personally don't like wearing headsets--but portable units are great if you like them and they will go anywhere you want to carry them.

be comfortable

Be as comfortable as possible. Unless you have a thing for freezing your butt off or frying your brain, I recommend exercising in the most ideal conditions possible--whatever that might be for you. Granted a walk outside on a clear, cold day can be quite invigorating. Do what feels good at the time and take care of yourself (see below).

take care of yourself

Take care of you! It's your body; you're living in it right now and you need to listen to it. Soreness is different from injury. Take time to heal yourself if you get injured or sick. Right now you have an incalculable number of days left to get where you want to be.

Getting Started (Cont.)

❦

How do you spend those many minutes doing the everyday tasks of preparing yourself for work? If you are like most of us, your mind slips into over-drive and mostly ignores whatever it is you are doing. And too often we tend to let our minds worry/fret/stew over all of those important things that are happening today, in our lives, to our "potential" futures, etc. I would like to recommend two primary ways you can make the most of this time:

Remember how to enjoy?

There was a time, and there were probably special times, when the mundane chores of getting ready in the morning meant something. See if you can remember when:

I'll start with an easy one: taking a shower. Even though I usually shower after I exercise and that is not always in the morning, I love to take a shower. Ninety percent of the time I relish the feel of the water cascading over my body and that wonderful feeling of getting clean. I don't always relish the idea of getting into the shower, but once I am there I almost always enjoy the experience, and the times I don't are usually caused by being in a hurry. Believe me! If you have ever been in a situation where you couldn't take a shower for a period of time (for me it was military survival training), you can **really** appreciate this ritual.

Now think about all of the other things you do in the morning, from going to the bathroom to shaving to putting on deodorant, cologne, make-up. If you pay attention to them, they actually are pleasurable--sometimes quite pleasurable.

For instance: I like shaving--it makes me feel clean, more attractive, more awake. If I pay attention to my shaving I find that I have a certain ritual--starting in the same place, going around in the same pattern, etc. Every once in awhile, if I am paying attention, I can get creative with this and try some "daring" new pattern.

Pay Attention!

The things we do in the morning all have a purpose. Paying attention to them at least some of the time helps us be more alive with ourselves, more in-tune with our physical being, and helps us remember, also, if we make the effort, that there was a time when we really did enjoy this. [Remember the first time you shaved, used makeup, used deodorant?]

I recommend that you pick one thing out each morning to pay some attention to. I think you'll be surprised at how it changes this small part of your day. Even if you don't always pay attention to these small morning rituals, doing so every-once-in-awhile does wonders for your psyche.

I also recommend that you vary your "rituals" and see how this little bit of creativity enervates your "boring patterns." You might even find a better way of doing something.

Take a Chance!

And for those of you who relish consistency and patterns in your lives--take a chance! It might really be hard; you might struggle the first time to change that ingrained habit and comfortable way you have gotten used to, but I think, if you make the effort, that you will discover that there are other ways of doing things that work, too, and just might make life a tad more interesting.

Try paying attention tomorrow morning to which sock you put on first. If you're like most people you have no idea, but you probably do the same one first every day. Now that you're thinking about it, it will probably take you months not to pay attention to it. (Sorry, you'll probably curse me for bringing this up, but it will get you thinking and paying attention!)

Diversion Three: Think positive thoughts

❦

Mornings, and particularly "getting ready time", are times when we tend to obsess about all the things we have to do, worries we have, what the future holds for us and our loved ones, the stock market, etc., etc. If you're anything like me, you tend to over-think things--build them up in your mind, mull them over forever and sometimes worry about them even to the point of literally making yourself highly agitated or sick.

If you have problems with this, I highly recommend that you get and read Richard Carlson's book **Don't Sweat the Small Stuff...and it's all small stuff**. This wonderful book has many, many suggestions about how to approach and think about certain things in life. The sub-title of the book is "Simple Ways to Keep the Little Things from Taking Over Your Life." It's available in paperback and is a great book to wear out with repeated readings!

I have tried to approach a solution to this problem of obsessive thinking from a number of perspectives. Some of these are also mentioned in Carlson's work. Keep reading:

Keep a big picture in mind

Really try to *keep the big picture of your life in mind*. Almost everything, when taken in context to your whole life, the world, the universe is "small stuff." And even if it feels like "big stuff" it probably isn't as big as you think at the time. A helpful exercise is to think about how this particular worry really impacts who you are and what you want to accomplish in this life.

What do you want to be able to say about yourself when your life is over?

I have often used the following exercise with my students and clients: draw a time line and put on it your birth, every event you think was significant in your life to this point, every major event you want to happen in your life from this point on, and a time when you will die.

Try to be fairly comprehensive and if you wish, set it aside and come back to it a couple of times for revision.

Then ask yourself at the very end of this exercise "what you would like to be able to say about your life when it is over (alternately you can ask, "What would I like people to say about me when I am gone.") You might also want to look at all of the significant things you put down up to this point in your life and then try to remember some of the things that seemed incredibly important to you before but for some reason just didn't make your list when you wrote it.

When I did this exercise my "answer" was: "I want to know how to love fully and be able to say that I am a loving person."

I found a great quote once that reflects this: "the only thing that matters at the end of my stay on earth is how well did I love, what was the quality of my love." This is a paraphrase of this quote. I carry it around in my wallet all the time. I can't remember where I found it, so I can't give credit, but I thank the person who wrote it because it really gives my life meaning and direction.

Obsessing!

I'm not going to pretend I don't still have trouble with obsessing about things I have to do, worries or concerns about my job, etc. It is probably the one thing I need to work on the most. I think a many of you will find you do this a great deal, too! So what else can you do?

tell yourself to stop!

Another suggestion is to just shout "stop," "quit," "cool it" to yourself and then make an effort to change the direction of your thoughts to a more positive direction. This probably sounds ridiculous, but believe it or not it does work!

Have **patience**! It does take time to make improvements. There tends to be a great deal of slipping back into old habits, but if you keep at it you will notice that you catch yourself more and more often and that you are more and more successful at interrupting this chain-thinking and replacing it with more peaceful, calming thoughts and ideas. I now almost immediately catch myself when I start this type of chain thinking and I can almost always nip it in the bud.

go ahead and think things through

I'm not going to tell you not to think things through. To tell you the truth, I find it extremely useful in my job as an administrator to work through these things in my head. I frequently run problems through my mind and try to find the best possible solution. Most of the time I try to give a serious worry or concern several days to resolve in my mind. Usually in that time I am able to think of some much better solutions than I would have by reacting immediately or giving in to obsessing about it.

The difference from my previous bad habit of obsessing or "chain worrying" about everything is that I try to **stay as calm** as possible (even if it is something that directly involves me and tends to upset me) and I try my best not to dwell on or continually go over the same ground. If I can keep my perspective and stay in control, my solutions usually include several of the ***Eleven recommendations for a better life: love others, be kind, be honest, be patient, listen, be creative.***

write it down!

This is one of my favorite ways of dealing with obsessive thinking. Especially if something keeps bothering me to the extent that some of these other techniques aren't working. I have been known to get up at three in the morning and go to the computer to write out in great detail something that is bothering me.

It could be just my thoughts, a letter to a person to iron out a problem, or even an essay on what I am feeling. The important part is getting it out where you can look at it and consider it. This helps to solidify your thoughts and take away the emotional charge attached to it. This also gives you the opportunity to revise and restructure your thoughts in a concrete--non-circular manner.

Try it! You might be surprised how much this can help.

Incidentally--I rarely print and even more rarely send these notes or letters to anyone. It's just my way of getting a handle on it.

talk to someone you trust

Worries, concerns, all types of problems can be helped by **talking to someone you trust**. It's amazing how someone else can give you not only a new perspective, but the support you may need when concerns arise. Re-member **"share yourself"!** Some of your problems, concerns, worries can be interrupted and re-focused through sharing. Two people can also be a lot better at brainstorming solutions then one.

And its a great deal less lonely.

Diversion Four: Time to Eat

❦

At some point during the "getting ready phase" of your morning you will likely "grab something to eat." So let's take our third diversion here and discuss ways to make the most of this part of our lives, also.

I love to eat! Most of us probably do. The problems arise in balancing our enjoyment of eating with all of the voluminous amounts of information about how we should eat, what we should eat, when, where (?), how much, etc. Well, I'm not going to repeat all of that wisdom and lore. You probably know a great deal already, and if you want to know more you can easily pick up a wide variety of source books and in-formation on what's good for you, etc. etc. etc.

This isn't going to be a discussion on vegetarian diets versus meat-eating, carbohydrates versus proteins, or which mega-doses of vitamins to take.

This will be a discussion of you: where you are at and where you want to be.

Listen to your body

The first thing to do in considering diet is to take a close look at yourself--remember the mirror test above?. Well, this is a similar test, but it starts more from a different premise--**How do you feel?**

Really!?!

Do you feel great all the time? Or are there times when your body is trying to tell you something. **Listen to your body**! Pay attention to how you feel at different points in the day. That will be the biggest indicator of what you may need to pay attention to as far as your diet goes so you can adjust your eating habits to feel great all the time. At the same time we want you to enjoy this part of your life also, so we have a balancing act to do here. How can you balance eating so that you feel good about enjoying what you are eating?

This IS important! It is a big part of life.

Your body is probably telling you a great many things throughout the day about what you should or should not be eating, drinking, taking. If you are experiencing highs and lows, bloated/gassy feelings, poor health, etc., you probably need to adjust something.

Professionals can help

Knowing where you are at may take some additional work, not just paying attention to your body: to start with you should **seek advice from your doctor** and possibly a nutritionist; you may want to study your eating habits; get more information on healthy eating and vitamins, supplements; and so on. I urge you to take this part seriously and get good information from reliable sources including your doctor.

It's your body

My body has been telling me all kinds of things since I really started to pay attention to it. One thing I have discovered is that I tend to eat too much at evening meals and almost never too much or even enough at other times. This has not been easy to correct! Old habits are hard to change, but this is one thing I have recognized and have begun to work on because when I overeat I pay for it afterwards in several ways.

What is your body saying to you?

Where do you want to be and how do you get there?

Okay you've determined where you are-- where do you want to be? And! what will it take to get you there?

Again this may need to be a realistic perspective. If you have diabetes or other serious health concerns, you have certain things you really should be doing. However, I believe, you CAN balance your needs and good health with enjoying eating. Read on:

diets

Sorry--I realize this word has all kinds of negative connotations, but I hope you will see that there are ways around everything. One thing you can do is continue reading below. I would also like to recommend a book, which offers a unique perspective: Sondra Ray's **The Only Diet There Is!** If you have been struggling your whole life with a weight problem or perceived weight problem these are the best answers I am aware of.

eat what you like!

BUT.....! That's probably going to be your first reaction: **But!...I...**

Since we are not being negative here, let's find another solution than giving up all those things you like to eat. You'll need some help and part of that help is:

be creative

Today you have access to the most amazing foods and cuisines ever! Try something new...experiment in the kitchen...if you love food this is well worth the effort, especially if you do have specific dietary concerns.

As one example: if you are currently battling every morning with bran cereal or high-fiber muffins, or other sources of high-fiber, you are not alone. I truly believe that if you are struggling through eating something you detest that you are doing more harm then good. What a lousy way to start your day!

What else can you do? Get creative and try different things. Nobody said you had to eat bran cereal if you don't like it. There are many alternatives and I bet if you work at it you'll find one or more you do like.

If bran or high-fiber is something you need in your diet, explore all the different possibilities: You can eat a wide variety of cereals/ bars; drink high fiber mixes or take high-fiber pills if you can't stand the cereals; eat fruits and/or vegetables; etc. On several occasions I have made high-fiber graham crackers by substituting bran for some of the flour--they were yummy!

If you don't know enough about fiber, find out and then experiment with different things. If some types of fiber bother you, try others. It is amazing the number of possibilities there are and how you can get creative with the possibilities. And once you start you'll come up with even more ideas and have more fun, too.

These ideas apply to many different things: low salt diets, high protein/low-fat; sweets, etc. Get creative and you'll find ways to eat things you like and still be healthy.

Check out your local health food store and try different things. Even our local supermarkets are stocking more and more "healthy" and tasty items. Try a wide variety and see what you like. You may also have to do some background research to find out what works for what you need.

but....I love chocolate

So do I....so enjoy it! Sometimes! Be realistic with your body. There are tons of things that we are often told are bad for us: big juicy fast-food burgers, sweets, cream/cheese/eggs/butter, alcohol, etc. My advice is to enjoy these things--but be honest with yourself and intelligent about how much and how often. I love these things, but I also love lots and lots of healthy things, and if I eat healthfully most of the time I can "splurge" once in a while. I am a firm believer in enjoying life.

make a list

Make a list of all the foods you love (if you want to separate them by those that are good for you and those that are not or those you think are not good for you, that will be helpful, too). If you really work at this you will find there are a great many healthful foods that you do enjoy and with some creativity you will be able to come up with many ways to make those foods that "aren't good for you" more healthful.

I was pleasantly surprised just recently when I tried some "baked," low-fat, potato chips. I actually liked them better than the fried variety. Today we have so many choices that we can turn a great many of our bad choices into good ones by simple experimentation.

try new things

This is you being brave! Take a chance and try some new things! There are a myriad of new foods and ways of preparing foods out there that really weren't around ten years ago. There are specialty meats with high protein and low fat: venison, ostrich!, turkey; much leaner cuts of beef and pork; lots of new vegetables and fruit; "exotic" spices, sauces, and on and on--all available at your local supermarket.

Try some of the new low fat things--don't stop at just one example. I tried several low-fat sour creams (I LOVE sour cream!) Before I found one I liked--and I really did like it!

Try ways of preparing food that are lower in fat, sugar, salt but just as tasty! (There is an advertisement on right now about using chicken broth for mashed potatoes instead of butter-- and instead of whole milk use skim--you'll have to be pretty good to tell the difference in regular and healthy mashed potatoes).

Try some new spices--I was given a blend of

several peppers (not spicy) that is good on almost anything and can help you reduce your salt usage. There are many blends of traditional spices out there today, too: pepper and garlic, lemon pepper, etc.

Pay attention to your food

Wow! How many times do you eat and not even realize you've come to the end of that burger and fries, or whatever you're wolfing down. Try to take some time to actually enjoy your taste buds again. If you do this you'll **slow down a bit** and probably just eat healthier because you **are** paying attention. If you are eating things you like, take some time to savor them. This can be a great part of your day!

Slow down a bit

This goes with enjoying your food. It also helps you to eat less and therefore more sensibly. It helps digestion immensely, too.

chew!

As a teenager I was once subjected to (through the "assembly" program at our high school) a man who practiced yoga. He could do all of these cool twisty things with his body, but what stuck with me from that presentation was one thing he said--that we should chew every mouthful of food thirty or forty times. [The reasoning he gave was that we need to mix the food thoroughly with saliva for digestive purposes.] I urge you to try this a couple of times. You'll find out that we rarely chew our food more than 10-15 times and often even less. If you chew a mouthful of just about anything thirty times it will be really, really disintegrated.

Now--I have never chewed my food thirty to forty times, but recently I have made an effort to chew it more like fifteen to twenty times. My reasoning is that I pay more attention to my food, enjoy it more, and I'm exercising!

Yup! I just said chewing is exercising. It is! AND if you do this you will very likely find yourself eating less because it takes more time to pay this much attention to eating your food.

If weight is a concern, try this!

Don't* eat anything you don't like!

*Sorry to use the big "D" word, but since it comes as a double negative it works out here. Alternatively I could say: **Only eat things that you like**, but it just doesn't have the same impact. This is something you're **doing** for yourself.

I mean it! I made a rule for myself about two years ago: **I don't eat anything I don't like.** Why should I? I can't think of any reason to. Maybe, if I was starving, but then I might find I liked it (whatever it is), just because of the situation. Why waste your life.

The old adage, "Waste not, want not" is a good one, so if that bothers you, then plan ahead. Don't make something you don't like; if you are going to dinner at someone's house it is okay to tell them what you like or don't like to eat. **Be honest**--after all it is the best policy! On the rare occasions that I go to a buffet, I always try a tiny bit of something that I think might be questionable to my palate before I decide to load up on it. Think ahead.

Making new habits from the old ones

In order to change bad eating habits go ahead and try following some of the suggestions above: find out what you want to change, look for ways you can change it, work on it **gradually** unless you are good at this cold-turkey stuff (after all you want to start a new habit--a better one--and stopping something cold turkey might just set the stage for another bad habit to take its place), **be kind to yourself and love yourself--always**. Changing a bad habit into a good habit may take some time. Be patient with yourself.

For example: How can you stop over-eating if that is one of your concerns--one of the things you really want to change? Remember that is one of **my concerns**--over-eating in the evening.

This is a tough habit to break in this country because many of our restaurants seem to cater to large appetites (We have even managed to influence many ethnic restaurants this way! Think of the many buffets we have available today--American, Mexican, Chinese, Italian, Indian, etc.)

My work has been toward gradually easing back on my evening meals and trying to eat more sensibly at other times (I tend to skip or skimp at other meals and find myself starving at supper time). I also have begun to separate dessert (if I have it at night) from my evening meal by at least an hour.

Another example of my effort has been in avoiding buffets most of the time. I still splurge sometimes, but I also eat more sensibly when I go to them. It certainly doesn't hurt me to eat less; I just need to "learn" a new habit. I'm not winning with the old habit; that's for sure.

Paying attention to my eating and enjoying what I am eating helps, also. I think one reason we tend to over-eat is because we are so busy not paying attention to these wonderful sensations, that we keep wanting to eat more because the few brief glimpses we do pay attention to aren't enough to satisfy us. Think about it!

Vitamins, minerals, supplements

I'm not going to give any specific advice here, just a suggestion. If you try anything, do it sensibly. Talk to your doctor, visit a nutritionist or other specialist, and read the literature. Find out what is right for you. I think it pays to be cautious and it also pays to try things out to see if they help--i.e. test the water before diving in.

And:

One additional suggestion: after you have checked all of the above, when you try something new, again: pay attention to your body. Your body will tell you if it is helping.

Mange'

Eat! Enjoy! Balance your needs with your desires and you will have a good day.

Getting Started (Cont.)

We will spend a good deal of time throughout this book discussing various aspects of relationships. One of the most important relationships for you, of course, is your family and close friends. Normally you would spend some time in the morning interacting with your spouse and children or possibly a friend.

We will spend more time on this later, but lets take another diversion to look at relationships in general.

Diversion Five: Relationships

Every day, with few exceptions, we are in contact with people. Sometimes these are people with whom we have very close and intimate relationships, sometimes they are acquaintances, fellow workers, and many times even strangers. How can we, under all circumstances, make these people a part of our perfect day?

If I were to sum this up briefly, I would say: reread the **Eleven recommendations for a better life** and then follow them. But let's look at some specifics. Later in the book we will look at relationships from the perspective of who you are interacting with (i.e. friends, relatives, intimate partner, co-workers, boss).

Be kind

This is always the best starting place for any interaction with other people and it implies in many ways **loving yourself** and **loving others**. I think it also implies **being honest with yourself and others**.

you make the choices!

Take a moment before you react to someone and make a conscious choice of how you will react. Actually think for that briefest of moments, what will this do? How will it affect them? Me? It doesn't take very long, and in that instant you can envision how what you are about to say or do will affect someone else (and yourself in both the immediate future and in the long run).

This pausing to think before reacting may be the best thing you can do to immediately improve your relationships, because in that moment of hesitation you have the opportunity to choose. The opportunity to choose being kind instead of being right (Dyer); the opportunity to choose being kind instead of angry; the opportunity to find a positive way instead of a negative way; the opportunity to change your response and hence the response of the person with whom you are engaged; the opportunity, in a very real way, to change your life, and quite possibly the life of the other person.

How would ---- react?

Another technique is to think of an important figure in your life--a religious figure, famous/respected person, etc.--and imagine how they would react. [Recently a popular item with young people has been to wear a small bracelet with the letters WWJD on it. This stands for "What Would Jesus Do"] You can use anyone you like or admire or who stands for how you would like to be as a person.

Take that brief moment and think about how that special person would react to this situation you are currently facing. It is amazing how much this can change your response.

Learn from others

Everyone can teach you something. They can teach you **what to do** and how to do it, and they can teach you **what not to do** and how not to do it. If you look at all of your interactions with people as learning experiences, you will have reset your whole perspective in dealing with others. This can really temper your reactions and drain off almost every potentially volatile situation.

Try it!

Learning from others also implies that you will make an effort to **improve your communications and your ability to listen**. Taking the time to listen will not only help you in your relationships, but will open up opportunities for learning many new and wonderful things. I am always amazed at how different people think and perceive the world, and it takes keeping my mouth shut occasionally to hear them and learn from them.

Observe

Watch what is happening. Watch the other person; watch yourself. By becoming an observer you step back from the emotion of the situation and make better, more intelligent choices. It is a very interesting perspective to have.

Be patient

We all make mistakes. We all get in bad or depressing moods. We all have days when things, no matter how hard we try, just don't seem to go right. One of our wishes when we have these moments or days is that other people will understand.

This should apply to how we perceive others, also.

Try to make an effort to understand where that person is coming from. Perhaps they have just had "one of those days." It can be a thousand things, and you could be just the person to help them start to turn their day or even their life around. This is such an important consideration that we will run into it several more times in this book in a bit more detail.

Be creative in your relationships

Creativity can add so much to all your relationships. If boredom is a problem in your life and some of your relationships try something else.

Don't be afraid to be the first one to take the plunge, either.

I hope you will see that throughout this book I keep urging you to explore new possibilities and discover new ways of doing things for yourself. Hopefully, the ideas contained in this book are merely the starting point for many of your own creative ways of dealing with life and all the wonderful and exciting people you are going to come in contact with (and if you really look hard--they can all be interesting, wonderful, and exciting).

You're Off!

❦

Whether you spend five minutes or an hour and a half getting to work, whether you walk, drive, ride a bike, or commute by train or other conveyance, and regardless of what time of day it actually is, there are certain things you tend to run into in the process of getting to work, and you probably have specific ways in which you deal with those things during the time it takes you to get to work. Let's spend some time taking a look at some really positive ways you can look at this time--ways that you can spend it meaningfully.

What have you been doing?

First, take a look at how you have been perceiving and using this time. Is this just another part of your day you'd just as soon do without? Is it a time in which you are bored, frustrated, anxious? Is this part of your day, part of a perfect day that you envision? If it isn't something you are enjoying, how can you make it something that you might even look forward to?

Ask yourself these questions now and then again the next time you are wending your way to work and see what you come up with. You'll find that paying attention gets you really thinking about times in your life that we just sort of let go by...."Opps there goes another half hour of my life...guess I didn't really need it or I would've used it better or paid more attention to it." [Doesn't this sound silly? Yet we all do a lot more of this than you'd ever think!]

Keep that Positive attitude going!

Hey! You've gotten this far in your perfect day and things are going great! Let's keep that perspective and make some great use of this time. Try some of the following suggestions and dream up more of your own. Keep an open mind on how some things impact you during this critical phase of your day. After all, as soon as this part of your day is over you are going to jump into your work, and if you are upset, bored, pissed off, or in some negative frame of mind you will take that right in with you. Think positive--find positive things to do! You'll thank yourself and your colleagues will thank you, also.

Use this time constructively!

❦

Put yourself into whatever situation you usually find yourself in on your way to work-- how can you use this time so that you don't end up frustrated with yourself, someone else, or upset with the world in general?

Obviously how you use this time depends on how much time you have, so if you are doing a long commute on a train or in a carpool or even driving you will want to expand on anything below to fit your own schedule.

Using little blocks of time

This is my own personal, great time-saver and time-user and something I share with all my students, clients, and probably anyone who will listen. We all feel like we don't have enough time. It seems to be the nature of the American way of life.

So how do we make more time?

Use your time--even the little pieces.

Once, as a very fresh (as in new) freshman music major in college, I asked a senior music student how he found time to practice 4 hours every day. His answer was very simple, but also very profound. I have never forgotten his statement and it made a marked impact on my life: "I make it."

One of the ways you can "make" yourself more time is to use all of those many little blocks of time we tend to waste during the day: travel time, time spent at stop lights, time spent waiting in lines, walking places, sitting in offices waiting for someone, etc., etc. These suggestions apply to any time of day that you may find yourself in a "little-block-of-time" situation so keep these in mind throughout your day.

Here are some specific ideas:

think pleasant thoughts

Similar to what we covered above--avoid the obsessive thinking and focus on something positive--loving thoughts, peaceful thoughts, thoughts about your kids, wife, hobbies, etc, or even planning/dreaming about that fantasy vacation. It's a great way to spend your time on a short drive to work and you don't even notice those other irritating drivers or delays if you do this (we'll get back to these types of irritations in a minute). If you find yourself drifting into any negative areas, jerk yourself back to your focus on pleasant things--in time you will find it much easier to stay focused on things that make you feel good.

It does take practice!

meditate

If you're not driving (i.e. in a car-pool, on a train, subway, etc.), you can actually take your little piece of time and become relaxed and peaceful--it can be very refreshing. If you have practiced meditating and getting into a peaceful frame of mind, you might be able to do this quite readily and enjoy a five or ten minute or longer relaxation just prior to starting your day. This is especially invigorating if you are a morning person and you have already been up for awhile.

snooze

A sort-of extension of the meditation /relaxation idea above--go ahead! This is your life, your day, and your rules. Have a good snore. You'll be surprised how good this can feel and how refreshed you will be!

P.S. Don't drive and snooze!

study/read something

I keep a magazine, note cards (if I am studying something), book, or whatever between the front seats of my car and whenever I get stopped by a stoplight, traffic, construction, or whatever, I pick it up and read or study. It is incredible how much you can actually get accomplished in these **many** formerly irritating moments. Instead of feeling frustrated by these inevitable delays, I avoid the negative feelings and replace those with positive feelings of having accomplished something and I've enjoyed myself to boot.

In a short drive to work (mine takes fifteen minutes and has 10 lights--give or take) I can read a magazine in a couple of days, even a novel in a couple of weeks. I often keep this type of material really light in nature so it IS relaxing. At one point I had an "Opus" book (Berkley Breathed) in between the seats and I would read two or more "strips" while stopped at a stoplight.

I also, almost always, take materials with me when I go someplace where I know I am going to have to wait--unless of course I have planned to relax or meditate during that time or do something else.

work on something

Long or short travel times can be used to get work done, but be careful that you're not over-doing the work stuff. If it gets to be all work and no play and you're not having any **fun**, find a way to add something to this time to make it more enjoyable.

listen

Many of you probably already do this, but if you plan ahead you can make it special for yourself: listen to the radio, tapes, CD's, self-help tapes that are meaningful and enjoyable. Pick stuff that motivates you, relaxes you, or just plain feels good.

cell-phones

This is something I haven't gotten into, so I can't speak to the value or validity, however, if it is a part of life for you, I'm sure it can be valuable to use during this time-frame. However, please be careful if driving and using a phone. Getting yourself-or someone else dead or injured probably doesn't figure into your idea of a perfect day.

Call someone special for a pleasant change from work-related calls and make their day (and yours!).

portable computers

Great fun! And almost a necessity for many of us today. I urge you to remember, though, that computers can be fun as well as work. Try playing a game or writing, and later sending, a loving or cheerful e-mail along with all that work you are accomplishing! Or! Write a poem! start that novel you've always wanted to write! "Scribble" in a journal. Get creative!

enjoy what's happening around you

Yes, I know you've traversed this path to work many times, but when was the last time you truly looked at it; paid attention to it? Once in awhile it can mean something to really look at what you are passing and how it impacts your life. Perhaps you will discover something that is useful to you or just something nice that you hadn't noticed before.

I am always amazed at what I learn when I pay attention to things. There is something that always crosses my path (or I cross its path) that adds significance to my existence. Try it. Pay close attention and see if I'm right. I bet something will have an impact on you or relate to your life either that day or later. Be patient and be observant and you will notice more and more of these "coincidences."

Wayne Dyer talks about manifesting things in your life....Focusing and meditating on the important things you want to have happen in your life. And if you believe that **you** make your own life and that your own living of life dictates how and what happens to you, then he is right. I just find that paying attention to things yields amazing benefits and coincidences. What you pay attention to can lead to some really interesting manifestations, coincidences, or happenings for you. And its fun, too.

Dealing with Frustrations

Many of us find driving in traffic, dealing with crowds and even individuals, and many other "obstacles" that we come across in our daily commute (or elsewhere) very frustrating. Some of the suggestions above can help immensely with these problems, but lets consider some other specific things we can do to stay positive.

First, you may already be getting "frustrated" with all of this "positivity" and perhaps you are thinking that to be so positive for so long sounds like exhausting work. You may be right if you are in the process of "learning to be more positive." However, it quickly gets easier and easier the more you get the hang of it and you'll also notice how much better you feel and the people around you feel. So stick with it! And smile!

I'm in a hurry!

It happens to all of us: we're behind, traffic's awful, an accident slows everything down, and so on. Tempers flare, horns blow, and suddenly we're on edge and have become Darth Vader of the freeway.

And our day was going so well...

Accept! That's the best advice I can give. Usually there isn't much you can do about it. Getting upset and frustrated will do amazing things for you, but they're all negative. So deal with what you can deal with and accept the rest. Stay relaxed and consider doing some of the things above to stay relaxed and to enjoy yourself.

Also, keep the BIG picture in mind. As early as two hours from now, this delay will probably mean nothing and even if it does, you can deal with it. You're smart, on the ball, and creative--find a solution. If you missed that important meeting...a day from now, a week, five years, at the end of your life, this delay won't even be remembered.

Somebody's being a jerk!

We've all been cut off in traffic; treated rudely and inconsiderately; felt like we have been treated unfairly, just generally feel like we've been stepped on, battered, and bruised. These "incidents" are frequently very difficult things to deal with and to get over. They reach to the root of our frustrations in life and dredge up our worst feelings, and often associated with past wrongs we feel we have been dealt. How CAN we deal with these kinds of situations?

the BIG picture--again?

You bet! How much does this problem really matter? Go back and read the part of this book where I talked about what you want to be able to say about yourself when you are done with this stay on earth. Is your reaction one that fits that perspective of yourself? I know, from experience, that these are often very hard emotions to deal with, but the facts are--you can turn them around with some hard work. It does take some time, though, and if these feelings are really deep-rooted you may want to get some professional help.

Perhaps you can relate to this: I get REALLY upset when I see people treated badly or put down. My initial reaction would be to be very angry and to charge in and set things right, however, I am learning to deal with those emotions and to get creative in how I react to such situations.

it is YOUR choice!

The most critical thing to learn from the very beginning is to see that YOU have a choice of how to react. Once you see that you have a choice, you have already made the most important step toward changing your self and your reactions because you have stepped back and begun to observe yourself and the fact that you can make choices. If you still choose to get upset, angry, or whatever, at least you have made a conscious decision rather then just reacting. NOW you can work toward learning other responses and making other choices. Keep at it; it does improve with time.

You may even, at this stage, get upset with yourself because you still feel angry, upset, frustrated when you find yourself in these situations, but that means you are making progress. You are making more and more important observations about yourself. Eventually, if you keep at it, you will see other choices; see yourself making less extreme reactions; you'll even find yourself making neutral or even positive choices occasionally. Then you are well on your way to turning this all the way around.

Wayne Dyer has a comment that I mentioned briefly earlier in the book, however, since I like this statement extremely well, it is worth expanding on here. So thank you Dr. Dyer: "When you have a choice between being right and being kind. Choose being kind." I have extended this somewhat with, **"If you have a choice between being positive or being negative--always choose being positive."** This is a great, GREAT! way to look at the world and especially a great way to deal with the people you come into contact with.

This might be very hard for you when you first try to put this into action, but it sure does work. I know some "always right" people who are very easy to fight with, but now I just let them be right while I try to be kind. I know from experience how hard this can be; but keep at it, because the results are amazing.

I have very few fights anymore.

We will get back to this later, because it is an important issue. How you respond can really make or break your day!

they are probably having a bad day

It's amazing how trying to understand another person's viewpoint changes your own. Perhaps that person who just cut you off or bumped into you or shoved ahead in line was yelled at by his wife just before he left the house, or has a big meeting that he is very late for, or is facing cancer surgery tomorrow, or maybe he/she was abused as a child--there are millions of possibilities why he/she is doing what they are doing and probably none of them have anything to do with you personally.

If you honk your horn or say something nasty, you are not going to help his/her day, or yours, for that matter. If there is some way for you to be nice to that person who is obviously having some difficulties YOU might just be the catalyst to turn that person's day around. At the very least you can avoid making their day worse which is a very positive something you do for yourself and the rest of the world.

It's a funny thing that we often play God without having the All- seeing, All-knowing ability that we attribute to God. The truth is we don't know what is motivating someone to be the way they are being at any given moment. **Be kind. Be positive.** It pays huge dividends and it really doesn't cost anything.

Think about it!

they're having an "idiot" day

Okay, time for a little humor. I mean it!

I really do....How many times have you done something really stupid that accidently "hurt" someone else? Something you said; something you did (like swerving in front of a car, bumping into someone when you're in a hurry, etc., etc.). You feel like an idiot, right! You didn't mean it. You would never hurt someone like that intentionally. And now you probably feel like a complete jerk, but inevitably it is next to impossible to "take it back."

It's hard to take back an "idiot maneuver."

So what do we usually do? We hurry (or slink) away. Trying desperately not to draw further attention to ourselves.

See that guy rushing away ahead of you. Boy I bet he feels bad!

So, if you think of the person who just did whatever to you, as being in one of those incomprehensible states where he/she just couldn't quite get it together--i.e. they just pulled an "idiot maneuver,"it does sort of take the edge off, doesn't it. Think of it as if the poor person's just having an "idiot day." You can even take this a step further and follow up your initial humor by imagining what this poor person is going to do next (be kind and gentle in your humor).

make a joke out of that incident!

Making light of something that normally would really piss you off is a great way to turn it around. I started doing this when I had my kids and they were spending more and more time in the car with me. Instead of swearing at someone who did something not so courteous to me, I would shout something much less volatile, like "You toad!!!"

This soon developed into all kind of "Toad" remarks and eventually expanded into other humorous reactions with my children. Once when a guy pulled into a parking spot I had been waiting for, the old "You toad!" came out and from that day until this my son, daughter and I still joke about almost anyone on the road who "gets in our way" with statements like, "I bet that's the guy who took your parking place, Dad," or "Hey, that's the toad who took my parking place,"and many other variations. We have a lot of fun with it and it definitely turns those potentially angry reactions into

126

something completely different.

This person might need all the help they can get right now in life. Wish them well, instead of ill-will; say a prayer for them; send them love; be kind. It feels much, much better then a negative response and who knows, you might be the one person who can change his/her day or even life around by your example.

I bet you never thought you had that much power!

You do.

Think about it.

More humor

Have fun in the car. I do! Especially with my kids, but even by myself. We have a couple of hills near our house that have signs on the bottom of the slope just before you head up that read "Dangerous Hill." I started this with my kids and now whenever we have an uninitiated person in the car and we go past one of those signs, we all scream loudly as if we are scared to death. Believe me, it confuses the hell out of the passenger, but after we explain it; we all have a good laugh.

There are always ways to make humor out of mundane situations. Try it. It's great fun!

Work!

❦

Ask yourself these two questions:

Do you like what you are doing?

Are you having fun?

If the answer to either or both of these questions is no, then you have some work to do.

Try this exercise: See how many of the following types of situations apply to how you see yourself in your work environment and how many of them actually bring up some negative thoughts, worries, etc. Make up as many more as you can come up with. If some of these hit a nerve, be patient, we're going to talk about them. [If you think of situations I haven't and you really need help with them, send them to me and maybe I'll write another book dealing with as many as I can. In the meantime, think about what follows and try to apply the recommendations to any problems at work you may have.

Problems at work?

    The work you are doing.

    Your boss

    Your co-workers

    Your staff

    Workload

    Pay/Benefits

    Recognition

Now, one at time, let's see if there are ways to help with this part of your day.

Your job!

❦

Do you enjoy your work, your job? Are you just going through the motions because this is where you are at and you don't see any other feasible choices? If this applies to you keep reading:

You're not alone. Many, many people look at a job as **WORK**! You go to **work** because you are responsible to your family, spend your time at **work** so you can have all of these other things, and then hopefully enjoy life after **work**. (Remember in the foot note at the beginning of this book where I talked about the "work" of this book. Well, this is that other meaning--the negative connotation of work.)

If you don't enjoy your work, **that's a lot of time where you're not very happy**.

Well, I have this strong opinion that "work" should be **fun** amongst other things like a learning experience. So if you are not having fun and you are not doing what you really would like to be doing this whole chapter is for you.

131

Change

If you are not happy doing, what you are doing it is **time for a change**. It may be a change from one type of job within your current employment to another, or it might be a change to a new job all together. It also, if you think about it, may simply be adjusting some other things through suggestions offered below, so read on and then make an informed decision.

The real key is to examine the problems that are creating your unhappiness and then to make a plan to deal with them.

two basic choices

Okay, you have two basic choices: you can quit your job and find something you do like to do; or if that doesn't seem to be an option you can make this job one that you enjoy **or** at least make it so you like it better until you can get another one. Let's look at the first choice first.

Where do you want to be?

Try this creative imaging exercise with yourself: imagine yourself in the most ideal job you could have, or doing the most ideal thing you could be doing. You can even do this as a guided meditation if you want.

What do you come up with? What do you really feel you would be good at and would really like to do? If you come up with more then one choice that is fine. That gives you some options.

The next part of this exercise is to imagine how you could get there. This may entail schooling, making/saving enough money to start your own business, whatever. These are preliminary plans so you don't need to go into great detail, yet! Just try to get a good idea of what you would like to do and what it might take to get there.

If you go through this process you will eventually see what paths are viable and what it will take to get to your goal. You will very likely see that whatever you have in mind IS possible. Maybe not easy, but at least in the long term a real viable possibility--keep in mind that you have thousands of days left!

The next question is whether you want to make that effort and take those chances.

Yeah, But....

Yes, there are many excuses: "I don't have the time." "I have too many responsibilities." "I don't have the money." etc. Sorry, **no buts-- allowed!** Let's just see what the possibilities are. Who knows you may find a positive answer that you couldn't have envisioned before.

Take the first step

Planning: after you have determined a goal and envisioned the steps to get there, you will need to establish a realistic **detailed** plan including some extensive background research.

School

If you need to go back to school to reach your goal--find out what possibilities there are in your community/area and what you need to do to start the process. You need to consider costs, part-time versus full-time, amount of time it will take, how you will cover your other responsibilities, etc.

You may find out you can take courses at night or weekends and reach your goal. You may discover that there are all kinds of financial aids (scholarships, tuition waivers, assistant-ships, fellowships, grants, loans) that you are not only eligible for, but just the type of person they are looking for.

If this turns into a long term deal, so what. Keep remembering those thousands of days you have left! You will find yourself a whole lot happier if you are working toward this important goal in your life and you may find that your unhappiness with your current job is not so important any more. So if you can only take one course a semester to start with, that's a great start. Your momentum may build with time and you may find other ways to help get this accomplished (summer classes, correspondence courses, tele-courses, internet courses etc.)

Your own business

Perhaps your goal is to branch off and start your own business--something you love to do, a hobby, an extension of something you already know, or even just something you always wanted to try. Again, the first step is to plan, in detail, what it would take.

You will need to find out all sorts of information: start-up costs; training costs, if needed; building rent/purchase; utility costs; how to handle personnel issues, taxes, viability within the community. etc., etc. Sink your teeth into this stage and really know what you would be getting into. You'll even want to know what type of success rate there is for this type of business. Consider ALL of the things you will be dealing with on a daily basis. Comprehensive planning is key to business success. Many, many enthusiastic entrepreneurs fail because the skimp on this stage.

Don't be afraid to get professional help with planning in the area you are interested in pursuing. You'll be glad you did if you do take the plunge.

Once you have this information you can then make an informed decision on how you can get to the point where you can dive in and get started.

You may find that this will take some time, perhaps even years of gathering your resources and gaining the know-how to really make a go of it. That's okay because you'll be having fun with the process. If you're not, you're doing something wrong.

Remember always: love yourself, be kind to yourself, have fun. Oh yeah, and **be creative**.

As a matter of fact, you may just find that if you perceive your current job as a means to an end, you will actually find yourself working harder at it and enjoying it more.

Take the plunge!

However you decide to change from your current job to another job you need at some point to just do it! If you have done all the planning and really know the pros and cons for you and your family then go ahead. Carpe Diem! Seize the Day! Go for it! Even if what you do is simply to apply for different jobs in the same field you are currently in, that's a big step because you are likely facing major changes in your life, including moving.

Change can be difficult and scary for all

of us. One of the most important things to keep in mind is that this is your life and for the time you have left what do you really want to spend it doing? What you are currently doing? Or is it time to make this effort?

This is another one of those balance things (like eating what you want and staying healthy). A tremendous amount of our lives are spent "at work." Try to find a way for your work to "work" for you and your life.

If the thought of that much change is just too overwhelming then consider some of what follows. There are many choices to help you enjoy your work.

Start enjoying what you are doing!

There may be lots of different reasons you are not enjoying what you are currently doing. I cannot cover all of them in this book, but I hope I can give you some ideas that will help you move toward enjoying your life's work and hence a major part of your life.

It is quite possible that you are actually in the profession that you want to be in and doing the specific work that you want to be doing, but for various reasons the situation is not satisfactory and you feel that if some things would change or you could change some things everything would be fine.

And there is the rub: if you are waiting around for things to change, you are probably going to have a hard time finding happiness in your work. Because it is your effort and attitude that will effect changes that need to take place.

Let's spend some time examining some general ways that your work might be enhanced. I will get to some specifics later (as listed above), but the principles listed below apply to almost any type of job from factory to desk to construction to thousands of other possibilities. Check these over and see which ones you can use to help make your situation better.

Attitude

This is probably the BIGGEST single idea that can help you in any situation. Most of us find out the hard way that what we bring into a situation (work or otherwise), i.e. our general attitude, really affects how we think, feel, interact with others. So one of the real keys to enjoying your work is how you feel about it. And you are the only one who can change that!

The good news is that if you have been working on improving all of the things in your day up to this point, you should already be approaching your entry into the work place with a much more positive attitude, so all we need to do at this point is keep it going and to work on those reasons that work may not be your ideal situation.

There are many things that affect our attitude, one thing we haven't discussed yet, is "How you feel"....physically that is. Let's take another diversion here and talk about your health.

Diversion Six: Health

❦

Ask yourself these questions:

> How do you feel about yourself?
>
> How do you treat yourself?
>
> What is this dis-ease in your life trying to tell you.

Each of these questions relates to the other. Let's explore them in more detail.

How do you feel about yourself?

First and perhaps most importantly, there are many authors who have suggested that how you feel about yourself has a direct impact on your health. A **DIRECT** impact on your health. [I highly recommend that you read Bernie Siegel, Deepak Chopra and others as they go far beyond what I can discuss in this book--see glossary at end of book.]

This is a very important point. All of the things you have been reading about in this book--the recommendations, suggestions, ideas--**have to do with how you feel about yourself** in this spectrum called life. As you begin to feel better about who you are and how you approach the world, I believe, that you will also start to feel better physically. Do your work--your work toward your perfect day--and you'll find that all the aspects of life get better because you just plain feel better about yourself and about the world.

You may, at this point, have realized there is a lot of work for you to do. If better health is one of the benefits--just think how great this work is for you!

Are you having fun, yet?

How do you treat yourself?

How you treat yourself is directly related to how you feel about yourself. Much earlier in the book I discussed the concepts related to and the importance of how you approach food and exercise. Obviously these both impact your health a great deal but the same perspective applies to your health in general terms.

Loving yourself--the whole person--is the biggest part of being healthy. Treat yourself as if you are the most important person in the world--**because you are!** This is not elevating you above everyone else egotistically--it is being practical. You will be of little benefit to anyone if you cannot be, if you are not, the best person you can be--loving, kind, honest, healthy!, etc.

Are you taking care of YOU?

Taking care of you

Taking care of you means taking care of all that is part of you--i.e. your physical, emotional, and spiritual well-being. I believe all of these are intertwined and that it is important to work on all of these to be a whole, happy human being.

Some things are pretty obvious, but it's amazing how we avoid thinking about them and especially avoid doing something about them through the course of our lives. It is impossible to share with you specific recommendations for the many possibilities here, but a good axiom is to apply the "Eleven recommendations for a better life to each of these areas of your existence."

Let's look at a few specifics:

taking care of you: the physical you

Balance: food, exercise, good health choices.

Know your body: "Listen" to what it is saying to you. From a medical standpoint it is always important to catch things early. If you are paying attention to how your body speaks to you, you will notice much more readily when something changes. Pay attention to your body; it will tell you when something is wrong!

taking care of you: the emotional you

Know yourself! Observing what is going on in your own mind and with your own feelings is a major step in working with emotional concerns, upheavals, and in resolving conflicts. This whole book is about enjoying your life. If you are not, then find out why and work toward some resolutions.

Be willing to admit when you need some support: All of us go through emotional difficulties and even crises in our lives: death of loved ones, breaking up, depression, etc. Be willing to admit to yourself that these are times when you need help and be willing to go for it. This can be professional help from a competent and caring counselor, social worker, minister, etc., and/or a network of support you have with friends and relatives. This is part of loving you! You are the one person who can help yourself the most by letting others help you in your time of need.

Help others! One of the greatest emotional uplifts you can give yourself is to help others. It pays really big dividends and even if it is a struggle to get started when you are feeling low, you will love yourself for having made the effort.

Take time for yourself: Sometimes we are "at risk" emotionally just because of physical (or other) circumstances. If you are tired, PMSing, sick, etc., you will be more likely to have some difficulties dealing with even simple emotional concerns. Take time out if you have to, to get things back together. I know that the worst times for me are when I am tired or sick-- those are good times to have some space and time for yourself to recuperate. (P.S. That's what sick leave is for--don't be afraid to use it!)

taking care of you: the spiritual you

Whatever you believe and however you perceive this world, universe, and yourself spiritually, be true to yourself. Following your true path, who you truly are and want to be, will be the most important thing you can do in life.

Knowing yourself spiritually and really knowing and practicing what you believe is a critical element to our lives. Each of us, regardless of religion or faith, approaches life from some very fundamental, deep-rooted beliefs. Working with those beliefs on a daily basis--meditating, praying, contemplating--can provide a profound basis for your health, well-being, and enjoyment of life.

Spend time with the spiritual you.

Every day!

Being and staying spiritual and true to our beliefs sounds easy, but it is the hardest part of the whole process, because we let our egos, our physical problems, our emotional concerns get us off our path. Bring these three things together with your spiritual foundation and always return to those roots when the going gets tough, and you will lead a happier and more fulfilling life. Guaranteed!

What is this dis-ease in your life trying to tell you

Many of the gurus who speak at length about your health have a fundamental belief that illness or disease is actually "dis-ease" or "uneasiness," "not being at ease" in and with our lives. If you think about this concept you realize that there is at the very least some truth to this perspective and perhaps a great deal of truth.

Illness

When you are ill, it pays to examine your life for things that might be emotionally contributing to your dis-ease.

A good technique is to meditate or pray about your illness and ask the illness or your deeper self, "Why are you here," "Why are you a part of my life right now," "What is this dis-ease doing for me."

You may get some surprising answers to these questions and then you can not only deal with the illness, but perhaps the underlying cause(s).

be informed!

The more information you have the better you can make the right selections for your health concerns.

physicians, healers, counselors

Always get all the help you can and the best help you can. Medicine, psychotherapy, etc. might not be the ultimate answer to your disease, but they certainly can help. A good professional is trained not only to provide immediate care for your concern, but also support and recommendations for your future.

Get help! Do not be afraid to seek help from a professional. And be willing to get several opinions. As an example: a general practitioner might look at a back problem from one perspective, and orthopedic surgeon, chiropractor, acupuncturist, physical therapist, massage therapist, etc., from other perspectives. One might be more right for you than another. You may have to do some searching to find the **best** answer for your concern or problem.

Always get second, third and even more opinions if you have a serious illness or concern. Professionals are all different and one may see something or know something that another one misses. Make sure you cover the bases in treating yourself.

Surgery

Some of us are very afraid of any kind of surgery. It is wise to be cautious enough to get several opinions and as much information as possible when facing this prospect. If you and your doctor(s) have determined that this is the best direction to take, then I urge you to read one of Bernie Siegel's books (see Bibliography). However, here are some quick recommendations (some of these are expanded ideas from Bernie's books):

make this your surgery

You're the patient--make sure you are the focus.

Be comfortable with your surgeon. If you're not, find one you are comfortable with if at all possible.

Make sure he/she keeps you informed every step of the way. You have a right to know anything you want to about what is going to happen. You have a right to all results, a thorough knowledge of what procedures will be done and what this means to you in the immediate future and in the long term. Know what medications you have to take and why. Understand the whole process--admittance, pre-op, operation, post-op, etc.

Ask to have some music you love in the operating room. You are not restricted to whatever the surgeon wants. Music can be calming and healing. Even if you are "out" you will know its there--your ears don't go to sleep!

Remember that most doctors **will** make the effort to do what is important to you. But you will need to be willing to speak up.

establish a support system

Know **before** the surgery who is going to be there afterward for you. Not just for a day, but for the complete recovery time. Knowing that there are people who care is very important to your healthful recovery. Don't be afraid to ask for help.

get set

This means: be ready. Sometimes we avoid thinking about "bad" things that are going to happen and thus avoid what we need to do to be ready for this. Take care of the business you need to, so you are not running about the day before or worried during the time you should be focused on recovery.

think positively

No matter how positive you feel about this, and many of us don't feel positive at all when facing surgery, you can work on your own attitude:

Treat yourself extra-specially before the surgery.

Use imaging techniques to see the surgery going perfectly.

Use imaging techniques to see yourself as healthy and whole following the surgery.

Make (or have someone make you) a meditative healing tape and listen to it for at least two weeks prior to surgery and one week after.

If you have time, make sure you are in the best possible shape and health before undergoing surgery.

Remember that this will be all over soon, and you will look back and probably smile at your trepidations.

it works!

I just had a fairly major sinus surgery, and I did all of the recommendations above, plus had a "healing/meditative" tape made that focused on limited bleeding, limited swelling, and fast-healing. After my second visit back to the doctor (two weeks following surgery) he said that I was healing better than people who had had surgery three weeks before me.

And I ain't no spring chicken neither!

Chronic and Terminal Illnesses

Probably the vast majority of humans have to deal with one or more chronic (long term) illnesses in our lifetimes. From many, many sources: the most important thing you can do for yourself for these concerns (besides working with professionals as recommended above) is to work with your **attitude**. The more positive you are, the better chance you have to overcome whatever it is you are facing.

stay in touch with your spirituality

This is a BIG part of staying positive and maintaining an attitude of hope.

be at peace with yourself and the world!

For whatever reason you are where you are because it is the right place for you at this time. Be at peace with yourself as you work toward healing. Love yourself.

Listen to Mozart!

Cuddle a kitten!

Love a child!

imaging

Work with positive, healthy images every day. Meditate or pray while imagining a healthful you. Many cancer patients today are taught to work with specific imagery exercises in dealing with their cancers: e.g. images created by the patient of destroying the cancer with white light, seeing healthy tissue, etc.

Imagine yourself as healthy, fit, and strong. Whatever image of yourself is the most positive. Keep at it! (Review the section earlier in the book about meditation and imagery.)

never give up hope!

There are too many unexplained remissions and healings for me not to believe that anything is possible. Hope and your own positive spirituality are the fuels that make miracles possible.

get support!

Sometimes when we are ill we avoid the most important support base we have--our friends. Or--you may find that because of your illness, your age, or other reasons you no longer have a support base.

Get one!

There are many, many wonderful people in the world, and many opportunities to establish support when you are in need: churches and ministers (You don't have to be a member and most ministers won't even try to "sell" you on their church or religion. They understand your need.); hospice programs; service organizations; even your neighbors. They can't help unless you allow them in. Don't be afraid to ask. You'll be glad you did.

Love and caring are great healers--for both the person who is ill and the person providing the support!

Find out!

❦

It is important to know what it is about work that is not fulfilling who you are and what you need to be happy, alive, and positive. Do the following exercise:

Take the time--I would recommend doing this for at least a week--and list all of the things about your work situation that you are not happy with. Be very specific. Even if it is something as simple as who makes the coffee, or how your electric pencil sharpener is cleaned. Keep adding to the list all week and be as comprehensive as possible.

If you find out and know what is bothering you, you can start to work on making changes. You can also start to build a larger picture of what the problems really are. You may find that all the little things are simply symptoms of some larger issue (e.g. I don't like my boss-- see below), and that if the larger issue is resolved these little things will take care of themselves.

Really take the time to do this and it will pay big dividends. It is fine for me to say to you "adjust your attitude, be more positive, and everything will be fine," but we all know that that type of generalization often leaves us with a good feeling for awhile, but nothing to fall back on when the situation keeps rearing up and biting us. Knowing the specifics helps you deal with the specifics and then you stand a better chance of not falling back into the same ruts.

Probably the biggest reason for writing this book is related to the paragraph above. Many self help books give wonderful suggestions-- probably most of the general ideas I have covered and will cover in this book are covered many times in other books, but I know that it helps me to see these ideas and principles applied to specific problems and concerns. While I can't get so specific that I am addressing your own specific items/issues, I hope that what I can detail will help you apply these successfully in your own life and work.

Love yourself/Be kind to yourself

❦

Why do we seem to forget these two very important principles when we step into the workplace? We seem to have this strange capacity when we work, to put our true selves away for the duration and then we try to find ourselves on the way home. Find a way during your workday to do things for yourself. I like to think of this as "warm fuzzie" time.

Warm fuzzies are anything that makes you feel better. They can be pausing for a nice deep breath of fresh air, patting yourself on the back when you do something good, treating yourself, taking a moment to close your eyes and think pleasant thoughts, stretching, or just noticing the world around you for even the briefest of instants, or any of a thousand other things.

I can't remember where I came up with this term, but I do remember one Christmas six or seven years ago when things were not going so well for me that I just up and decided to buy myself a warm, fuzzy Teddy Bear.

Silly? Maybe. But I hadn't had a warm, fuzzy, stuffed animal in many, many years, and it did lift my spirits, and I am not ashamed to say that there are times that it still does--just seeing it on my bed can bring a smile to my face.

Give yourself a warm fuzzy once in awhile and smile--you are definitely worth it!

Give warm fuzzies

Warm fuzzies for yourself can also be doing warm fuzzies for others.

What a great way to put a little brighter glimmer into your world and others'. Smile, be friendly, say something nice, give a treat to your assistant, bring donuts for the whole gang, help someone who is having a bad day or is just behind...whatever feels good.

[An assignment I have often given some of my students and clients is to make an effort to give five warm fuzzies to different people in a day and to note, in writing, how they reacted. One of these people has to be a complete stranger, i.e. a store clerk. Wow! They are always surprised at how much of a positive impact it has on others AND themselves.]

Again...Pay attention

Seems simple. But paying attention to **what we are doing** and **to the people we are working with** can make a great deal of difference in how we perceive our work. Since we've talked about this before (see "GETTING STARTED!") I won't belabor this. We do tend to get into ruts in our work, but by paying attention we do a better job and feel better as a result.

Other people will probably notice, too!

Be the best you can be

The old Army recruiting axiom applies to your whole life! If you're doing it, and make the effort to do it well **for yourself,** you will enjoy doing it more.

This is very important.

We spend far too much of our lives trying to please everyone else.

I've been making a concerted effort to take notice when I do a good job such as congratulating myself or treating myself when I do something well.

This may seem selfish at first blush, but it isn't. You are much more likely to take care and do your best when you are striving to "be the best you can be," than when you are striving to look good in someone else's eyes. This orientation or perspective focuses your efforts on who you are and what is important to you.

Too many other factors come into play when we rely on approval from others. You can fight others' elevated opinions, jealousy, egos, etc, if you want, but it is a losing battle. There is no way you can control all of those extraneous factors and no way you can control, **ever**, other peoples thoughts or feelings about you. **If they haven't discovered love and acceptance yet, than the best you can do is to teach them by example.**

Aim high for yourself; feel good when you accomplish things. You're worth it!

Love/be kind/be honest

This is the best way to change people that I know of. Anything short of this approach **will not work**.

It may take time, but your positive attitude in approaching work and others will make significant changes in your whole approach to life and often, as a result, in the other people around you....Try it. You may have to work at this...and it will take time. You will also have to be very, very patient, because what is important is **your** attitude, not someone else's and whether they are changing theirs. That's just a bonus that frequently comes along with your own effort.

You might even want to take a chance and ask someone how you are coming across, because we really don't see ourselves as others see us. (I did this once and what a revelation!) Ask them to be totally honest. It is often quite surprising because, for example, we may think of ourselves as business-like, direct, open, and honest. Yet, our co-workers might see us as stern, depressed, and uncommunicative. If you find out that you are coming across differently than you imagined, you can then make some adjustments. "Know thyself!" (Socrates, I think.)

Also, take some time to think about how you do want to come across. Then you have something to aim for. "If you want to be loved, be loveable." (Somebody said something like that some-when.) Or think of the old Chinese proverb: "If you keep a green bough in your heart, the singing bird will come."

Be creative

I can't tell you how to be creative as there are zillions of ways, but I'll give you some suggestions.

First of all, get over that notion that you're not creative. I once had a student tell me she was not creative--my answer was quite dramatic and not to be repeated here. You are creative if you can think. It's one of those things that separates us from the lower animals. You may not think you are artistic, but if you tried you might find that you have a streak there, too. You really will never find out unless you are willing to take that first step.

Brainstorm--whatever. At work you can brainstorm new ways to do things and perhaps come up with a suggestion that will change things a great deal, or maybe just a little bit. Change keeps us alert, alive, involved.

Change your workplace, etc. Many creative things may have to be tempered to your own work environment, i.e. what is "allowed", what will fit, etc. I like to take reasonable chances, but if you feel more tentative and if you aren't sure about something, ask....and keep asking. If one thing doesn't fly, try another. I've found that there are ways around just about everything. Sometimes it's a great deal of fun finding those paths!

Your inspiration may just trigger others to do things as well, and maybe (likely?) your work place will be more alive. Ask others for their ideas--get a brainstorming session going. You may find that a problem that has been impossible to solve will resolve itself through dialogue and ideas from others, and they will appreciate being asked.

Many, many good things can come from creativity. Make sure you think things through relative to your situation before jumping in, but if you can find ways to dive into being more creative at work you will enjoy yourself and your work a lot more.

Help/encourage others

Impromptu efforts to help others or spread some general good cheer in the workplace can pay big dividends. It's so much better than being grumpy and isolated. You'll like yourself a whole lot more, too. Try it!

Learn

I love to learn--anything. If I could impart this wonderful feeling to all my students, I would be an ecstatic educator. Since I work at a University, I have lots of opportunities to learn right at my work place, as a matter of fact I earned one of my degrees while teaching full time at a University. Anything is possible if you set your mind to it and the gears in motion.

A close friend of mine had a job she enjoyed very much, but the job was static--no where to go without more education. She has recently taken the plunge to go back to school part-time, so she can have more opportunities for advancement, pay increase, etc. It was a very hard decision for her because of time, finances, responsibilities, etc. But I know she will enjoy it and benefit from it.

Every job has learning opportunities. Find out what they are and how you can benefit from them.

You can also learn from your fellow workers, your boss, and learn from what you are doing. Get out of the stasis mode and into an active mode of learning! It will help you to open up and probably open up opportunities for you.

There are also ample opportunities for learning in your community. Take some time to find out what they are and how they might impact your job.

Cultivate your garden

As mentioned at the beginning of the book, this sort of goes along with learning, but is more a nurturing of yourself. Find ways at work to nurture who you are and who you want to be. Experiment with ways to use your work environment to enhance your life: I tape some sayings, my children's art work, and pictures to my door, wall, desk and change them every once in a while. They help to remind me what I am working toward and what is important to me. They also let others know what is most important to me.

Surround yourself with things that help you to be you: this is easiest if you work at a desk, but outdoors you may want to carry some special item in your wallet, purse, or tool kit. I often write or tape things to the backs of credit cards and keep sayings in my wallet. Also, I have seen people with pictures and quotes taped to the insides of their tool kits.

Nurturing can also be relevant to things that you wear, how you fix your hair, etc. Make a statement. Yes, you will find that there are often some restrictions in a work environment, but usually there are ways you can be creative and nurture yourself at the same time.

Take a break

It's amazing, but there are a great many people who never take advantage of those coffee breaks, lunch breaks, etc. Work seems to take precedence over everything and everybody-- including yourself.

Take care of you!

Are you a workaholic? I am, but I have recently made the effort, and believe me it is at times a major effort, to give myself a break.

Those little breaks during the day can revitalize you and make you more efficient (not to mention likeable) on the job. I have already given many suggestions earlier for using those "little blocks of time" so you may want to revisit some of those suggestions. The important thing here is to take advantage of those times when you have them. Even if all you do is wander about the office and say hi to a few people.

We workaholics do have to make an effort at this. I am one of those people who struggles with feeling guilty if I haven't accomplished something constructive in a day (hour/minute?). Even when I am home, on weekends, during vacations. Often when watching TV I tend to be doing something else. (Of course, this is a great time to get things done as the TV really doesn't require your full attention.) But if you are like me it is tough, very tough, to just sit and do absolutely nothing. There's always that nagging in the back of your head that something needs doing.

Fight it!

Take some time with and for yourself--take some time with and for others (**share yourself**).

Treat yourself to breaks. You'll find that you're happier and people around you are happier.

Think about it.

Take a vacation

When is the last time you really took a vacation?...for yourself--not for others?...Just to do something you want to do, to be where you want to be or with someone you want to be with, not someone who you feel obligated to be with?...Time off doing something that has absolutely nothing to do with work?

Whoa-a-a--if you're a workaholic its probably been awhile (ever?)

I travel a great deal, but it's almost always associated with work. Now, I consciously try to set aside times when I go do something for myself. Sometimes this is by myself; sometimes it is with my family and/or others I WANT to be with. The important part is that I leave work behind and go.

It's also important to occasionally do something totally for yourself and by yourself. These don't have to be long periods of time, a day can do wonders! Though taking a longer "by your self" vacation every once in awhile is a good idea, too.

Be patient

It's very hard at times to be patient with bosses, fellow workers, and others we contact at and through our work. Try to keep in mind that we all make mistakes, and this may just be one of those days. Patience pays off big dividends over time. It shows the world that you are loving and kind.

And I know that I really want to be that way for the world!

Lunch time!

❦

I hope you remembered to take your breaks!

This is the **BIG** break. Make sure you plan for it and take it. It is a very important time for you to get rejuvenated.

eat!

Something.

relax!

Have fun!

balance!

Remember to balance what you eat (your health) with enjoying eating (Are you having fun yet?).

fast food?

Probably the most difficult time to truly balance what we eat from a health standpoint with enjoying what we are eating is during lunch-time. Our nation's eateries are geared toward providing fast service for their customers as the primary focus. Often, unfortunately, they seem to ignore both the healthfulness and quality of the food we are offered. Luckily over the past five to ten years there has been some move toward improving both these areas in the fast food market, but you have to be careful, wise (knowledgeable), and often plan ahead.

bring your own

What has happened to the old lunch box or brown bag? You can have some very pleasant short lunches if you plan a little bit ahead and bring what you want to eat from home. It is very likely to be more enjoyable, more healthful, and you can choose a very comfortable place to eat (outdoors?!)

It's your life--find the balance.

enjoy

Even if you only have fifteen minutes for lunch, and sometimes in spite of our best planning that's all we can squeeze in, take the time to enjoy what you are eating. Everything said in the "breakfast" section ("Diversion Three: Eating") applies here.

If you don't like it; don't buy it and don't eat it!

There are plenty of good, healthful alternatives today. Take some time to find those you enjoy. Believe it or not most of them are quite reasonable in price as compared to everything else.

Smell the roses

If you have a half hour or more set aside for lunch you will likely have some time to do more than just eat. Take that time to do something for yourself. Many suggestions have already been given, but here are some reminders:

Take a walk and enjoy the flowers, etc.

Close your eyes and rest.

Talk with someone special (call them?).

Read (for pleasure).

A good time for warm fuzzies (see above).

Play a game of checkers, chess, or whatever.

Have a nice laugh with someone.

Your boss

This would be a good time to go back and review what has already been said about relationships in Chapter "Getting Ready" and recommendations above. Then let's go ahead and try to look at some things you can do to help out with more specific concerns.

If you otherwise like your job, but you have some issues with your boss and this is a major sticking point toward your enjoying your work, then this section is for you.

I'm not going to get into the psychology of your childhood and attitudes toward authority here. If you think that's a concern then I recommend that you seek professional help. What we CAN do here is take a look at approaching bosses in general and see if there are adjustments that **you can make** to help the concerns you have.

This is a key point, because you are not going to change your boss and his/her attitude toward you unless you change. **Accept that fact, because it is all important.** You may be well-meaning and even right about how you feel and react to your boss, but the odds are he/she isn't going to appreciate your being right. They will almost always appreciate you're being kind.

Be positive: always

Most of us learn the hard way, and there are some people who never learn that **negativity never helps**. That is well worth repeating over and over to yourself in BOLD PRINT: **NEGATIVITY NEVER HELPS**! If you are going to solve relationship problems you need to make positive adjustments that will effect change in yourself and through your own personal changes potentially you may effect change in others.

At all costs avoid the negative.

Be positive: always!

It is worth taking some time and thinking about this for a few moments. You may even want to meditate on it. I urge you to take a break from reading at this point and actually think about any situation you want to. Try and see if you can come up with one where being negative would have any kind of positive effect. It probably wouldn't even make you feel better to yell at your boss, because while you might have the satisfaction of having told the ol' SOB off, the deleterious effects will likely be long ranged and long remembered.

It's not worth it!

Negativity is never worth it.

It is also important to remember that you are dealing with a person's ego and at times, as you probably know, egos can be pretty awesome to deal with. Be kind, be gentle, be loving--those are the keys to change.

Be Patient

Helping the whole situation between you and your boss may take some time, you may have a long history to erase, and you may be trying to change someone's perspective of you whose attitudes toward you are deeply ingrained. Your effort should be aimed at changing yourself--if that helps to change someone else, great, but always aim at what you can do, not what you are expecting others to do. The person you are dealing with may never change and eventually you may have to face that and go about your own business as much as possible within the constraints of the relationship you have with them or to seriously consider looking for a better position with someone you do feel comfortable with.

In the meantime use the above recommendations and those that follow and anything else constructive you can think of to make the situation the best that you can.

First of all, consider many of the suggestions already offered above. They will help your overall attitude. Secondly, it helps to try to view things from your bosses' perspective. It may give you a better understanding of where you fit into the big picture at work:

Learn from them

You also should think of a very important aspect related to learning from others: I have learned a great deal from many people in life **and at least half of it came from people I really didn't like.** I think, hope, I am a better boss because I learned a good deal about how and **how not** to be an administrator from some of my previous bosses.

I believe we are in whatever situation we

are in to learn things, and we will continually find ourselves in those situations until we have learned the lesson we are there to learn. **So try to find out what it is you are supposed to be learning** in this situation that is bothering you. It might just be that you are to learn patience, kindness, love.

The really bright side of this is that once you have truly learned this lesson, whatever it is, you probably won't need to encounter it again in your life. I like those kinds of deals!

Assess the concerns

This is, as you expect, a part of almost every recommendation in this section. The specific problems you have with your boss (he's/she's too demanding, non-supportive, inconsistent, grumpy, etc.) will all make a major difference in what you may do to improve the situation. Temper the following recommendations to whatever you come up with.

Be kind and loving to your boss

Be kind and loving to your boss because that is just what he/she may need. Remember the time you spent this morning sending loving thoughts to someone. Why not pick your boss sometimes. This can be hard to do if the relationship is really strained, but try it. You'll probably start to relax a little bit, and you might find as a bonus that he/she does, too.

Do something surprising!

Do some kind, surprising thing for your boss when least expected: say something nice, give them a little gift, compliment them, ask them if you can help with something. Be creative. He/she might be suspicious at first, but if you keep it up without being too obsequious about it you might find that you are starting to feel better, and they will relax more in the relationship, too. Start slow and build.

Again, don't expect miracles. You may have a long way to go. Your aim is not to get a raise or change your boss's whole personality. It is to change your own perspective so you can enjoy work more.

Be willing to talk about it

This may be the most important advice I can give you about relationships, and it took me a long while to learn this. However, I found out that if you are willing to open up and address your concerns with your boss (or others), he/she will listen and try to understand you. Not all bosses will, but most will. In other words find a way to open up communications with them.

Being open and honest about how you feel may actually set in motion a whole lot of improvements in your relationship with your boss. He/she will probably be surprised at how you feel. He/she might not have any idea of your feelings, concerns, or your perspective of the relationship and the problems you are having.

It is very important that you do this from a positive, affirming, learning standpoint.

Try very hard to do this from your own perspective. For instance, don't say to your boss that he makes you feel unappreciated. Rather say that you would appreciate it if he/she would let you know when you are doing a good job as well as when you don't. You can even let him/her know that you appreciate constructive criticism, but are hurt when he/she doesn't offer an explanation or suggestions when you have done something not up to par.

Most bosses will respond positively to your efforts to "improve yourself" or your efforts "to understand." Try to couch things from your own perspective--always. Try to avoid any wording that might be accusatory. If you precede/set your comments with "**I** feel," "**I** am," etc., instead of "**You** make," "**You** are," you'll be much more successful.

Own your own feelings

Try very hard to do this from your own perspective. For instance, don't say to your boss, "You make me feel unappreciated." He can't MAKE you feel anything--you choose to feel unappreciated, hurt, angry, etc. Rather say that you would appreciate it if he/she would let you know when you are doing a good job as well as when you don't. You can even let him/her know that you appreciate constructive criticism but are hurt when he/she doesn't offer an explanation or suggestions when you have done something not up to par.

Most bosses will respond positively to your efforts to "improve yourself" or your efforts "to understand." Try to couch things from your own perspective--always. Try to avoid any wording that might be accusatory or will make the other person defensive. If you precede/set your comments with "**I** feel," "**I** am," etc., instead of "**You** make," "**You** are," you'll be much more successful.

You are your own success story

Your success is not calculated by your boss or anyone else for that matter. Be your own judge of what you are doing and what you are accomplishing. I know this is a very, very hard lesson to learn in life, but it is **your reaction** to what others say that sets the tone of your life, not **what they say**! Really think about this last statement because it is very important in all your relationships.

If I say you are a tree, you are not going to believe or accept that from me, because you know that you aren't. If someone says you are a jerk and a lousy worker, and you know you aren't, why do you accept that?

Yes, their words can affect us in many ways. A promotion, raise, even our job can be affected by someone in authority who gets down on us. However, keep in mind that that is them affecting the physical you, **not defining who you really are inside**.

You are capable of weathering anything that comes along. You've done it before. You are an amazing person and have many great qualities.

You can respond to criticisms

There isn't any reason you can't--just remember that negative responses will not beget anything positive. Be positive, open up communications, get support from significant others in your life. Turn this around through your own creative, positive response.

What are you learning from this?

Another perspective is that problems and concerns--and even tragedies such as losing your job--are sometimes what we need in life to help us change directions and move toward new and better things. It is your choice to make something from whatever happens--you have the chance to make positive choices or to make negative choices.

You have the opportunity to learn or not to learn from this experience.

Choose wisely.

Hopefully, if you work with yourself and some of the recommendations herein and others that you may brainstorm, "bad things" will be minimized and your whole situation can improve. It's worth the effort.

If nothing else works...

you may have to consider changing jobs. Not everyone can work together or for someone of a vastly different personality or outlook. Accept that life is not always fair. Not all people are the way we would like them to be, even at our best and most positive we may not have a major affect on someone else. Enjoy who you are and where you are at and if you feel a major change is necessary after all, check with the thoughts above about changing jobs and start planning!

Your co-workers

Much of what has been said about problems and concerns with your boss and the applicable recommendations are relevant to everyone you work with, however, the perspective is different. Your boss represents an authority figure and potentially a certain control over how and what you do at work. Co-workers tend to get on our nerves for different reasons. You will want to consider specifically what is troubling you about a certain person or persons. So....

Make a list, a detailed list, of your concerns so you have something to work with then reread the section entitled **Diversion Three: Relationships** and the entire section above about working with your boss. Then check out what is below--these are additional suggestions for different types of relationships in the workplace.

Communicate, communicate, communicate
and also
Listen, listen, listen

Reread the section above under "bosses" about **being willing to talk about it.** The **way** you approach a person is all important. With a positive, understanding approach you will be much more successful than with anything remotely negative.

Many problems in our relationships with co-workers (and others) stem from egos getting in the way. By listening carefully to someone else, even if you don't agree with them, you have given them a chance to be themselves. You may even feel they are terribly wrong about something, but your choices always come down to "being right or being kind. Choose kind!" (Dyer) Or as I like to expand on Wayne's statement--you can choose to be positive or to be negative....Always choose to be positive.

Unless you happen to like arguments.

Overbearing, criticising, domineering, demanding, annoying, pushy folks!

You know the type! Those individuals who insist on hammering their ideas and beliefs into you irregardless of what you feel and believe -- those inconsiderate types who are sure they have this pre-ordained mission to correct your misbegotten life and wayward existence--those people who can't seem to get through the day without criticizing you and everyone else. YOU! Yes, you, have become the focal point for their savior-complex.

Unfortunately, you already know avoidance doesn't work!

Help!?!

love them

Where they are currently in their existence is a result of many, many influences and experiences (just as your current place is the result of yours). You may not like who they are, how they interact with you and others, what they espouse, but you are definitely not going to change them through arguing and fighting.

Your best chance of changing anyone is through being an example of loving kindness.

Try this the next time you are "assaulted": listen calmly, patiently, and generously (believe me running away or being impatient won't help and arguing will just fuel the fires). It's surprising how often this is enough to defuse this type of pushiness. You don't have to give in to them in any way or agree with them. Ultimately any response you make should be as positive and affirming to them as possible without giving away any of your own truth and power. For example, "I really appreciate understanding your viewpoints better." And leave it at that!

If they continue to harass or make demands you have other choices:

stand up for yourself--lovingly

You have a right to your own space and beliefs. Sometimes you do have to play hardball, but always give the person a lot of room to maneuver when you do put your foot down.

As a specific example: I know a person who is very demanding and pushy--hates not having his own way and is one of these "always right" people. I frequently come into contact with this person, so I do have to deal with him.

My technique--always(and I learned this the hard way)--is to listen calmly and carefully, offer support where I agree, and offer alternative suggestions when I don't. If I have to make a decision that is antithetical to this person's perspective, I do so firmly and kindly: "I appreciate your input and enthusiasm, ----, but I feel I have to make this decision ....because...." or "I'm not sure we can really do that because....so let's try some different things," etc. Give them some space to maneuver, and they won't feel like they are "up against" you.

When you are as kind as possible about dealing with these types of personalities you have an excellent chance of standing up for yourself without great battles and arguments. Yes, you may have a slightly bruised ego to deal with, but that is far better then dealing with a major campaign of healing combat ego wounds.

use your head and your heart

When really troubled by a problem, a person who is being a problem, or both, always try to step back and take a close look at the situation before reacting in some way.

My favorite technique is to write a letter-
-usually a long letter. I will sit and work
through, on paper, those thoughts that I would
normally spend lots of time obsessing about. I'm
not sure why this works, but if I write it down,
and specifically address it to the person I am
concerned with/about, it really helps defuse
much of the emotions and often clears the way
for a much better, more intelligent and more
loving, solution.

Ninety-nine percent of the time I end up
destroying the letter.

Ninety-nine point nine percent of the time
if I just react I am very sorry afterwards: use
you head; use your heart.

really talk about it!

This is a bit of a reiteration of the section under "bosses," but slightly expanded. When
a person is "on your nerves" and just doesn't
seem to be willing to let you alone, then you
need to go to them and broach the subject.

This takes a lot of guts! At least the
first few times, until you see the value in it.

When you make the decision to do this, work
it out on paper if you need to or even with a

friend and then find the strength to go up to the person and make an effort to let them know that you are upset.

own your decision

Again the way you approach this is all important. Own this yourself--if you blame them they **will** get defensive, and you probably won't make any headway. **Blaming leads to defensiveness and gets nowhere.** Let them know that you feel a certain way because of what they are doing or how they are doing something and let them know you are seeking a solution.

Believe it or not, this alone, may be enough. Often people don't realize how they are affecting someone else, and even if they do know, they are astounded by someone who has the courage to come up to them and actually tell them they want to talk about it. They may back off right then and there and your problem is solved.

If they don't then you may have to set some guidelines for the relationship. Again, be as kind as possible.

an example

I wish I could cover every possible instance, but since there are infinite possibilities, I will try one example:

A fellow worker is taking advantage of your kind and generous nature and giving you a good deal of extra work that they should be accomplishing themselves. You've already tried saying "no," nicely, and that doesn't seem to have gotten through, and they always seem to have a way to get around that. It's time to talk--firmly/kindly.

Be willing to tell them exactly how you feel and what you feel the appropriate solution is. Give them some specific guidelines since they haven't accepted your "no" in the past. For instance: "I am willing to help you understand how these reports need to be written, but you will need to write them yourself." "I am willing to help you with some of your work, but only when I have completed my work." I will help you with any problems you have at four o'clock, but I need to get my work done until then." "I can help you with one project a week." "I will help you with this type of work if you will help me with this." etc.

be specific

If you need to, get very, very specific. Set up guidelines that you will accept and let them know what you will absolutely not accept.

Then stick to your guns!

I think it is Ann Landers who frequently tells people that they can only be taken advantage of if they let themselves be taken advantage of.

The first time you do something like this may be difficult. The second time a bit easier and so on. Just remember to be loving, understanding, and kind, whenever possible.

And don't be afraid to be you!

teasing!

Teasing is closely associated with what was just said--what we accept inside ourselves about what someone says about us **IS** our choice.

However, if you have a low self-image and no matter how much you try to shake it off, this stuff still hurts. Remember that change does take time and you have embarked on a wonderful self-healing journey just by reading this book. By making the effort to understand yourself better, to love yourself, you will find that all of this will become easier with time and perseverance.

Have courage!

Love yourself--be kind to yourself--always.

You deserve it!

It isn't any BIG deal!

Sometimes little irritants come from other bigger problems we are dealing with elsewhere in our lives. If the big problem is solved the little ones really don't matter much any more. If the big problem is a relationship: boss, co-worker, staff, then work on those and try to minimize or restructure the little things in life.

whose turn is it?

One example of this type of "little" concern is something like, "Whose turn is it to make the coffee?" There are lots of ways to deal with this kind of problem, and as we all know these things can escalate into all out war in an office. Read on:

do it yourself

Okay, it's not your job, or only your job every 4th week, but somehow you seem to end up doing it. So what. It can be your generous contribution to the stability and good will of the office. [And it's remarkable how good you can feel about being generous if you let go of all the negativity associated with "Whose turn it is" or whatever.] You might find that if you start doing it without the slightest hesitation every morning and without the slightest ill-will, that suddenly you'll have help, or someone will bring in cookies to go with the coffee, or you just feel better because you've given up on all that tension associated with the "whose turn is it?" syndrome. [And you might find you like your coffee better, anyway!]

help out

Set an example by helping out when little problems or concerns arise. You might even see how quickly you can find a way to solve the problem:

get creative

All these little problems have creative solutions--they really do! Train yourself to identify these small problems as early as possible and then train yourself to think creatively when problems arise.

If you're stumped, ask for help. Get a group together to come up with a solution. And remember the following: **voting is not always the best answer!**

Democracy is great if everyone is willing to go along with the majority, but as you know very well, that's not always the case. If you can find an equitable solution or acceptable compromise for everyone through brainstorming, that is far better than alienating someone or a group of people because the majority **won**.

If you do vote: try to make sure that everyone agrees to abide by the decision without prejudice, before you vote.

make it a challenge

It's surprising how much fun people can have if you re-frame a problem or concern into a game or challenge. You might get a whole department involved in solving a concern or minor glitch in the system if you get people involved in finding a solution by challenging them, dividing into teams, etc.

Make sure to keep it non-threatening and fun.

know your problem

While this is really implied in all of the suggestions above, it is worth stating: make sure you take a close look at what the concern or problem is. The process of observing (remember **synthesis analysis synthesis** from the **Guidelines?**) something from every angle often has a remarkable effect on finding a solution.

Staff

❦

Again, much of what needs to be said is found in the sections above on other relationships. However, being a boss has other connotations and responsibilities. I do not plan to write a long book right now (ask me again!) about how to be an administrator. These are just additional suggestions and extensions of suggestions found above to give you some insight into being a boss who can have a "Perfect Day."

Get to know them

Knowing the people who work for you can pay great dividends. They will also appreciate your attention and effort to know them a great deal.

walk the halls

I make it a point to greet my faculty every day. I always get up off my duff (usually situated at the computer) and walk down the halls and talk to the students, faculty, and staff. I try to do this several times during the day as it gets me up and moving and keeps me in touch.

Spend some time with them whenever possible. It pays dividends in many ways.

open your door

Often a boss is placed, by the nature of the position and the physical structure of offices, apart from everyone and frequently with at the very least one secretary and her desk in between him/her and the outside world. I suppose there are good reasons for this, or ostensibly good reasons for this, but I try to maintain an "open door policy." And I believe the faculty and students appreciate it.

I can always shut my door when I need privacy or instruct my secretary that there are times when I don't want to be disturbed. I have even set aside specific times when I do sequester myself.

By the way this is much better than doing it the other way around, i.e. "having times when people CAN come in to see you." Perceptions are important. If you have an open door policy and sequester yourself at certain times, that is much more positive than if you have a closed door policy and see people at limited times!

listen

Sometimes we think we don't have time, but if you are a boss you should make time. You can learn a great deal from your staff about who they are, what is important to them, how they see you, about yourself, etc. Listening pays great dividends, especially if you are listening to them as a kind and caring person.

Give them the opportunity to grow

Providing opportunities for your staff to learn new things and grow personally and pro-fessionally is a great way to keep things humming and keep the morale up. Learning is a fundamental aspect of human life--offering your staff these types of growth opportunities can be very positive and have a marked impact on productivity.

Even providing educational opportunities that are not directly related to their actual work can have a positive effect: CPR, human development, human psychology, etc., etc., wind-surfing, etc.

Did someone say wind-surfing?

Why not!

Judge kindly

As a boss you will eventually have to make many decisions that are based on different types of evaluations. This cannot be avoided and sometimes you have to make hard decisions and very difficult choices. Consider the following as loving ways to approach this:

do it yourself

When you have to make a hard decision, then you should have the guts to do it yourself. It is kinder, and it makes you think hard about all the different possible solutions before you make a decision.

be honest

Talk to the person directly, openly, honestly about what concerns there are. They may not be happy about what you say, but if you are open with them and kind, they will appreciate that and be much more likely to take your advice about improvements.

do it now!

Ninety-nine percent of the time, it is best to let people know where they are at and what concerns there may be as soon as possible. Putting things off builds tension in you and doesn't offer the person concerned the opportunity to work on the concern.

This goes for positive as well as negative feedback. As most of you probably are intimately aware, it is very frustrating not to know where you stand with someone. Any feedback is better than none.

be positive

Find the good in people--not just the bad. If you work well with people and make the effort to be in contact with them regularly, you can give them frequent positive reinforcement. This can really make the difference in someone's day and life.

You can't expect them to assume they know what you are thinking--good or bad and you especially can't assume that because you don't say anything that they know everything is all right.

Not surprisingly, if you maintain positive contact with your staff, you will also catch the concerns faster because you are in touch.

be specific

Always be very specific in an evaluation process about what the concerns are, how they might be addressed, and what you expect as a solution. This gives people the opportunity to make corrections and you might even brainstorm with them some ways of making improvements.

give them a chance

How many chances and how much leeway you give someone is up to you. What I mean is: offer them an opportunity to find a solution to your concerns. Let them know what the problems are and that they can make improvements.

If they are aware of your concerns, and you offer them a way to improve; chances are they will make the effort

If at all possible, get them involved with the decision you do make. Help them to be a part of that. If you empower them, they may take the initiative to make the corrections. It is very rare that someone does not care at all about how they are doing. They will make an effort if you give them the information and chance.

Be patient with change, also. Let them know that as long as they are making an effort and making improvements that you will work with them. They'll try even harder.

give them some space

Your employees may have ways of doing things that just don't fit into your own perspective of how things should get done or when. However, if they are getting the job done and on time, you may not have a concern.

It is really amazing to see what a little freedom can do in the workplace. Being creative and letting others be creative in their jobs can bring a whole new vitality to the "everyday grind." This has been identified recently by major industries, where we see more and more people allowed to work out of the home (particularly recently with computer skills) and more and more flexibility with work schedules because of commuting problems, childcare, personal preferences, etc.

Think about this advice seriously--it may solve some of your evaluation concerns, because your staff will be happier and more productive.

Treat them

Do something nice for your staff--not just at Christmas. Take them out to lunch on their birthdays or send them a personal note. Bring donuts in once in awhile. Talk to them when they seem down. Everyone needs warm fuzzies.

Be a person not just a boss: think about it.

Have fun!

Have some fun--who said work has to be serious all the time.

Cultivate your garden

Being concerned about your staff is very important.

Being concerned about *YOU* is just as important.

Learn to nurture yourself:

take that break!

Take time off, too. You deserve it; you've worked hard for it, and believe it or not the of-fice will maintain without you. It doesn't hurt to keep in mind what would happen if you were in a car accident and seriously hurt or a heart attack--would the world keep going? Would some-one find a solution in your absence--you bet.

Take that break!

Everyone--friends, family, staff, YOU, will be glad you did.

treat yourself

Us old farts need warm fuzzies, too.

you can learn something, too

Remember those "extra" educational opportunities you might offer your staff. Why not dive in yourself. I bet there are lots of things you would like to know and do.

Wind surfing sounds fun, doesn't it?!?

be ambitious...

About everything listed above.

About love:

"Rule" from love

Actually I like to think of an administrative position as a service position. I am a guide to help everyone stay on track and to keep things flowing smoothly. I rarely, if ever, think of myself as a boss.

I think if I, and those of you who are in or will sometime be in an administrative role, find a way to keep love in the picture--love of self and love of others--that we will do a good job.

Workload

If you are working too hard, it is because you choose to work too hard!

That may seem like a harsh statement, but it's very likely a true one. This life is yours to make of what you will; if you are working too hard you have chosen that path. If you don't like it then make some changes. There are many suggestions above that relate to this--here are a few more:

find out why

Take some time and really examine your life and particularly (but not exclusively) your work life and find out why you feel you need to work so hard. There can be umpteen reasons: **your** boss, your family, getting away from something or someone, money, etc. Try to identify the specific reasons. Then you will have a chance to make some adjustments.

I will discuss just a few to give you an idea on how to approach this, but there are already many recommendations above that apply:

your boss

If you are being overloaded with work and it is making your life difficult, you are unhappy, and it is affecting many other aspects of your life, the best thing you can do is talk to your boss (see above). This may be very scary, but it is this or change your job or your job situation in some way. Most bosses will appreciate your candor.

Just be sure to think it through, personally own what you are saying (i.e. "I need to make some changes in my job load because I don't get to spend any time with my family anymore." Avoid things like, "You are giving me too much work," which is blaming), be specific about what you can handle and how what you are doing is affecting you and your family, (be honest), and be willing to tell him/her how you feel and what you can handle.

money

Everyone or almost everyone thinks they need more money. The true question then becomes: what is the cost?

If the cost is your happiness, is it worth it?

If not, make some changes: this may include balancing income versus enjoyment in life, a job change (see above), and education (see above).

See below for some more suggestions under "pay."

getting away

Sometimes we work too hard because we are trying to get away from something or someone. We find work is our "salvation" from other parts of the world. The key here is to identify what it is that is prescribing our "overwork" and then to do something about it.

If you are a workaholic read the section above about "taking a break" and "taking a vacation." Take a close look at how your overwork affects your life and your enjoyment of life. You will find the answers you need and the ways to change from this process.

If you are trying to get away from a bad relationship then you really need to consider what the choices are. Some ideas are presented above, but we will hit this again when we talk about family relationships, so keep reading.

Pay

❦

You're not being paid enough for what you do and it's not fair!

You're probably right.

However, the choice is between moping around and being pissed off or doing something about it. If you're going to have a Perfect Day, eventually you will need to do something about it.

I have already talked at length about changing jobs and going back to school. Here are a few additional ideas:

Don't be afraid to ask

You have to have the courage and belief in yourself to ask for a raise. Sometimes it is as simple as that:

I knew a college teacher who, in spite of having a Doctorate and lots of great credentials, never got past assistant professor (There are two more levels up—associate professor, and full professor.) Mostly because he never made the effort. With a little effort he would easily have made it up at least another level.

Promote yourself

If you work in a big office, you may do a great job and never be noticed. Sometimes you have to help yourself be noticed. This is often just a matter of being friendly (don't hide behind your desk all the time). Make it a point to know and shake the hands of important people. You don't have to be pushy, overbearing, or obsequious about this. Bosses know brown-nosers from those who are just being friendly and a "part of the team."

A great part of this comes from just feeling good about yourself, and there is nothing wrong with feeling good about yourself and what you accomplish. So you don't have to do anything that is against your principles.

Educate yourself

Do some background research and find out if there are ways at work to improve your pay and/or job level through education. If there are, then find a way to start working toward that goal.

In addition, find and try other educational ideas on for size. I believe I mentioned above that I got one of my degrees after I had my doctorate and while working full-time as a college professor. I started the degree because I was just interested in the area. It ended up being a major reason I am in the job I have today.

You may learn something that you can use as a side business, or seasonal business. There are always opportunities, but you have to jump start yourself and get busy.

Benefits

❦

This is a tough one, because many times we don't have too many choices. On the plus side many businesses are starting to offer their employees a variety of possibilities: HMO's as well as standard health insurance; choices of deductibles and levels of coverage; life insurance options, retirement plan options; etc.

The most important thing you can do for yourself in relationship to benefits is to "**get educated**." Find out what is best for you and your family. Think both short and long term. Dive into all the literature you can get your hands on and compare, compare, compare. Make the best, most informed choice you can.

Ask around!

When I have interview for jobs, I always get as much information as I can. I make it a point to ask not only the people interviewing me, but also the people "in the trenches." They really know what the different coverages are and how the different plans work. Don't be afraid to ask! You will be glad you did.

Accept!

Sometimes I think that some things in life are put there for us to practice simply accepting. We can't fight everything, and we can't change everything. What is that wise saying that goes something like, 'Change what you can, accept what you can't, and be wise enough to know the difference!"

Someone also once said, "You can't fight City Hall." And there is a great deal of truth in that statement, too!

When it comes to benefits, it doesn't hurt to let someone know what your needs are and what you would like. Always be willing to, in a positive way, express yourself. You may or may not effect change--a great lesson in life **is** to know what to accept and be peaceful with it and yourself. I wish you peace! Always!

Recognition

❦

We have all probably, at some point in our work history, felt neglected, unappreciated, unrecognized, left out. Work makes up so much of our world and takes up so much of our time that **how we feel** regarding our work is really crucial to our existence. This is probably one of the biggest reasons we don't feel good, and why we don't enjoy our work. Let's explore some recommendations to help:

Pat yourself on the Back!

Why is this so hard for us to do? It seems like we really feel like we are being some egotistical snob if we congratulate ourselves for doing something well. I'm not talking about getting a swelled head and bragging to everyone--just a simple, "Hey, you really did that well!" to yourself.

Unfortunately we rarely even allow ourselves that! Too often we are finding fault with ourselves even in our best moments.

Do you tend to kick yourself and berate yourself regularly? Is this really who you want to be?

You have other choices: accept yourself, validate yourself, love yourself, treat yourself as God's child!

Say, thanks!

Are you one of those people who always finds an excuse when someone congratulates you? Is this familiar: "Hey, Joe, I really loved what you did with that contract." "Yeah, but, I didn't have the time to...." Somehow you always manage to negate the positive comments of others! (Remember the "**Yeah, buts...!**?")

Learn to accept congratulations and praise graciously without putting yourself and your work down: "Thanks Bob, I really appreciate your saying that. It makes me feel good." (And it will if you try this!)This is a hard lesson to learn if you are like the person above. Start working on it and after awhile you will find yourself feeling better about your job and you!

Recognize how good you are!

    Chances are you wouldn't be where you are now if you didn't have what it takes. Take a few minutes each day to take a close look at all the things you have accomplished. We so often get lost in the bustle and hustle of work that a whole day goes by, and we can't even remember what we did at the end of the day. Take a brief moment sometime and think about all of those myriad of problems you dealt with, all of those interesting people you met and helped out, all that "stuff" that seemed so important at the time. You did it! You survived and you're still hail and whole.

    Hey! You're good!

Do your best!

    Wherever you are and whatever you are doing, if you do your best, you should feel good about yourself. Long ago I read most of author Ayn Rand's books (**The Fountainhead, Atlas Shrugged**, etc.). One thing I remember from them more then anything else is that the characters, whether they were building great skyscrappers or flipping hamburgers--did their best.

We all make mistakes and we all feel bad about that. Move on. Do your best. Dwell on the good you do and the many positive things you accomplish. Love yourself.

Don't be afraid to ask

When I started my current job, one of the things I said to my boss was, "I would sincerely appreciate your letting me know whether I am doing a good job and let me know immediately if I do something wrong so I can work on it." You should be getting feedback. If you're not and you are losing sleep over not knowing--don't be afraid to ask. You can't deal with what you don't know.

Awards

Awards and other types of formal recognition are nice, but they don't determine who we are and how good we are. As you know all too well, frequently these things are more political than truth in recognition.

Accept yourself for who you know you are

221

and these things become far less important.
Accept yourself for all of your good qualities
and build them inside yourself and share them
outside of yourself with all others and very
likely, when you least expect and when you
probably don't need them any more--you will find
recognition and rewards.

When you are a person who always works and
dwells within a framework of traits like the
"Eleven recommendations for a better life,' or
any other list that is meaningful to you, then
you will be your own recognition and people will
know you for who you truly are.

Going Home!

Wow! You made it through the day. You're probably tired, hopefully content with how things went, and ready to unwind. However, as you know very well, you still have things to do, people to interact with, and a Perfect Day to finish. There are some very important things left to your day, so hang in there!

The Trip Home

We covered the trip to the office pretty well, so there's not a great deal more to cover. However, there is one key element that has changed--you are probably tired. I don't know about you, but I am well aware that when I am tired I am most open to "losing it." So the best advice I can give here is:

Recognize where you are right now!

Before you jump into the car (bus, train, etc.) to head for home be sure to take a brief moment to take stock of yourself. Knowing how you feel, how tired you are, will be the best tonic you can give yourself in making the trip home safe and enjoyable, i.e. keeping in tune with your positive day.

Then, if you are just starting this process, remind yourself of some of the suggestions in the earlier section of the book about getting to work. This will help put your mind into gear for dealing with all of those potential frustrations "on the road."

Make the most of your time in the best way that you can.

Take some time for yourself

Two minutes with your eyes closed and of deep breathing in your car can work miracles before you head out from work...Or try a short walk, five minutes relaxing in the office NOT DOING ANYTHING except relaxing after everyone has gone, or any other non-work related,

Side trips

❦

If part of your "routine" in returning home from the office is stopping at the cleaners, supermarket, hardware store, or other minor diversions you should also consider ways to make these detours a part of your continuing Perfect Day.

All those people you meet!

Through the course of a single day we come into contact with many people in a cursory sort of way. Often the contact is extremely limited: a passing glance, a greeting, an exchange at a counter, a brief remark, etc. While these types of "communication" seem to be of little importance to our lives, it is surprising how much they can change our day, AND if one makes the effort to be positive with all the people they meet, they can change the day of those people, also.

The following recommendations apply to any time of day; however, since we frequently have these brief encounters when we are "off running errands," I think this is a good time to discuss them.

Make the effort

Far too often when we engage someone briefly we are focused inwardly and pay little or no attention to them and who they are and how they are doing. If we pay attention and make a little bit of effort, we can keep our positive day going and very likely add to, if not completely turn around, their day.

The little things count in life!

Make contact

Just making eye contact--the willingness to risk that much of yourself--and nodding acknowledgment of someone else's existence can be a big positive step. People appreciate this type of acknowledgment. It's almost as if when someone is willing to notice we exist that they are affirming who we are and that we are valuable as a person.

effort the easier you can find things that are good and attractive in others. You'll find yourself liking the world more; you'll find yourself liking yourself more.

It's amazing what a little love can do!

Try it!

"All we get are complaints."

Sometimes we do need to make people aware that the service/products we have received are below par. If and when you need to do this, keep in mind that there are **kind ways** to say things and offer constructive criticism and very unkind ways.

Try to find the kind ways.

If you have made an effort to be nice and friendly, it will be far easier to share with someone your concerns, and they will be much more likely to accept your comments.

Here's one example: Let's say that a waitress in a restaurant has just delivered a steak to you that is too well done for your tastes. First of all it is not likely that this is her mistake. Secondly, if you bring this up to her, gently, she will more than likely bend over backwards to correct the problem.

Remember a long way back in this book I said I don't eat anything I don't like. I always send food back at a restaurant if it is not correct or not of the quality that I expect--I just try to do it kindly. It is amazing how many benefits this will have for you--most waitresses, managers, etc., will really try to make sure you are satisfied, and they will appreciate your efforts to resolve the concern in as positive a way as possible.

Most people really don't like conflict!

If they don't respond in a positive way, you might reconsider many of the items mentioned in the section on "going to work." It just might not be their day; they may be having a terribly difficult time in their life right now; they might be sick or very tired, and so on. If you stay positive, chances are you will eventually have a positive effect and remember--**negativity NEVER helps**.

Sometimes it is very hard to stay positive, but it is worth the effort!

Change your direction!

Make sure that somewhere between the office and home, you leave the office behind. My recommendation is to do that as soon as you step out of your work place. Soon you will be home and a new world is there for you to be with. It is pretty likely that those two worlds are separate enough that you don't want to dump one into the other without good reason.

Family

❦

When you arrive home you will be stepping into a world that probably is vastly different from your world of work. We are going to look at the important familial relationships you have in your life and yet, the recommendations included can be applicable to any significant people in your life. This is a good section to get creative in. If you have been working through this book, by now you will have garnered some good practice in being creative. So get busy and use your new talents!

In the door

Just before you step through the door into your house, take the briefest moment to assess yourself again. If you find any tension, over-tiredness, or are just plain feeling "out-of-sorts," this would be a good time for you to have a "time out." You might even want to build a little bit of relaxation, rejuvenation time into your regular schedule at this point. Your family will probably be glad you did.

With a family you can make this a sort of special game or way of organizing a small aspect of the family life. If everyone has a "spot" and everyone's spot is governed by the same rules (these can be quite flexible or more rigid depending on the dynamics in the family), there can be a true sense of peace and comfort in knowing there is a place you (and they) can be and not be disturbed.

Honesty is the best policy

❦

All your intimate relations need to be centered on trust and trust can only be built and maintained through open and honest communications. Whether you are interacting with your spouse, an intimate partner, your children, or a close friend, **honesty IS the best policy**-- always!

I believe, both from my psychological training and from my fundamental spirituality, that if we work on our ability to remain open, communicate as well as possible our feelings and ideas, and show who we truly are at the root, that our relationships will always be better....the best! The old statement of "Do what I say; not what I do," is very appropo here. You must be outwardly who you are inwardly.

It is very important for you to be who you say you are--to everyone.

I think this is particularly true in dealing with our children--and I will probably mention this more specifically below, but this is a good time to bring it up. Your children will learn far more from your behavior and your

Children

❧

You may not have children, but if you do
or if you come into frequent (or even
occasional) contact with children, this section
is for you. I can't cover all of child
psychology here and certainly will not even
attempt to cover all that I wish I could, but I
think the general recommendations listed below
will help in most circumstances. Remember that
professional help is available if you are
dealing with an over-whelming situation. Also
remember to always go back to the most
fundamental guidelines you have; your own list
of "Recommendations for a better life." (I hope
you have been busy by this point in revising mine or
making up your own!).

Love

[All of what follows really applies to our
intimate partners as well. As you read you might
want to apply it to both your children and your
spouse.]

This **IS** it! The one rule you can count on

all the time with children. The one basic
principle that should be the most important
thing you consider every time you interact with
children.

It is amazing that while many, many parents
feel great love for their children, far too many
don't show it. Maybe they don't know how, or
maybe it is just awkward and difficult for them.

If this is you, **"GET OVER IT!"**

I don't mean this negatively. I mean you
have to get over that bump. The awkward-
ness/difficulty in showing how much you care--
that's the bump we all have to deal with
sometimes. Examine yourself carefully and see if
this *in any way* applies to you. If it does, you
have some work to do.

I grew up in a family that I would say had
great difficulty with showing affection. I have
seen it in many other families of close friends
and relations. It IS possible to stop this cycle
of neglect... and I really see it that way: not
showing affection is a form of neglect. In some
cases it can even be considered a form of abuse.

You get over this bump by working on it. By
working on you and your ability to show love and
affection.

Showing affection

We show affection in many ways, but the most important way is through touch. Touching can be very difficult for some people, but it is well worth the effort to get past those blocks. Hugs are one of the most wonderful forms of expression we have.

hugs

Have and give lots and lots of hugs for your children. Every day--hugs. Every time you think of it--hugs. You need them, too.

We had, still have, **family hugs**. The whole bunch of us get together and have a big hug. What a wonderful way to express the joy of being human, of being a family, of togetherness, of just plain old-fashioned--I'm glad you're here!

Hugs do that better than anything I know--They express the very positive feeling of, "Hey, I'm really glad you're here, because you make me feel good and I want you to know that."

Give lots and lots of hugs. Boy, will you ever feel good! And your kids will, too.

P.S. Don't stop when they get older. The frequency may go down or be tempered somewhat by sex/age/situation, but don't ever give this up. If you can, find someone to hug every day. If you feel awkward about it, ask: "Would it be all right for me to hug you?" But most of the time if you are open and huggable the hugs will come in and most people won't take it the wrong way.

P.P.S. It took years for me to get my Dad to hug--but now he has loosened up to it. It was REALLY worth making the effort!

and kisses

Kissing is also very special, and I have witnessed families (men, women, children, grandparents) all kissing each other as a form of affection. How pleasurable it was for me to see such openness and sharing within those families. As in hugging, these expressions given between all family members were simply a sharing of the feelings one has within a closeknit group of people.

How and to what extent you do this in your family is up to you. With my children, I kissed them on the mouth when they were younger (I have a boy and a girl) and while things changed as they, grew we still have some forms of expressing our love and closeness. My son is fifteen, and while we don't kiss we still hug sometimes. We shake hands or clap each other on the back, or share other similar forms of affection (like high fives!); my daughter decided at about four or five that she didn't like kissing my mustache, so we changed to occasional kisses on the cheeks or head and always a good night kiss!

the handshake

This sign of greeting and affection is perhaps reserved more for acquaintances, but if you have a teenager it might be all you get.

I like a handshake that means something-- think about what a handshake means to you and what you want it to mean to the other person. Just this small effort will very likely change how you shake hands.

Actually, I always liked the ancient handshake where men clasped arms rather than just hands. It sort of has a type of comradery feel to it, a more positive bond.

Giving

I will address this again in some detail when talking about intimate partners but giving to kids is special. It is special because we are not only expressing our love and joy in who they are, but we are helping to build their personalities and character. So here are a few recommendations for giving of gifts to children:

Give your children what they will enjoy. Children are amazing in their preferences when it comes to what they actually play with. Observe them carefully, and you will have a better idea of what they will play with for a long time versus those things which may be used for one day and then set aside.

Surprise them: Small little treats, given intermittently are a great way to show your affection.

Be practical: Sometimes you should be practical about giving gifts--things they will have fun with and learn from, and once I've said this I can add:

Be silly, too: Be silly in your gift-giving, too. Laughter is good medicine.

Be creative: Some of the best and warmest gifts we can give our children are something we have done for them. Find a way to do things for your children--you will feel really good about it. They will know, even if they don't show it, that you made the effort. They will remember. **They will remember forever!**

Do it yourself: always! Find a way to be intimately involved in giving yourself. It will bring you great joy and your children will know and appreciate it for the rest of their lives.

Spend time with your kids

This goes hand and hand with loving your kids, but also with discipline and everything else dealing with children. When you spend time with them, they will know you care; they will know that their well-being and growth are important to you. Today is the time to start. You can spend time with your kids every day, even in broken families the children are only a phone call away (fax, e-mail)!

I can assure you that no matter how much time you spend with your children; you'll wish you had spent more! They ARE that much fun to be with!

There are a number of types of really important times with your children besides holidays:

things you like to do

By all means do some things with your children that you like to do. Introduce them to fishing, working on cars, knitting, etc. etc. This is part of learning, and they may continue to do these things with you, or they may not. That's not the important issue--the important point is that you are sharing who you are with them--you're not shutting them out.

things they like to do

Most of the time, maybe even all of the time, **if you try it--you'll like it.** Some of the best times I've had in my life have been trying things my children wanted to do. Try their adventures on for size: like going to a water park or playing Nintendo or having a tea party.

Family time

I'm not sure why, but family is very important to me. Just the basic concept of a family and the closeness that thought engenders. I think that finding some times, even if they are only several times a month (and that may be a miracle with teenagers) to spend as a family are very important. The time can be a wide variety of things from meals together, church, outings (picnics, movies, miniature golf, visiting a nursing home, etc., etc.), to family games and so on.

As one example from my college days that I still remember quite fondly: I don't remember who or quite when this "tradition" started, but when most of us were older (college, just out of college) we had a brief span of years where we would gather at Thanksgiving and have the "Koob Annual Thanksgiving football game." To tell you the truth it was more pitiful than anything, but we had a great time, with lots of laughs. Those are the types of images you will treasure forever!

Have some laughs

Find a way, every day if possible, to have some laughs with your children. I have already illustrated a few examples previously in this text, but here are a few others.

One thing that grew out of a George Carlin performance I attended with my son was related to something I did with my kids from the time they started going to pre-school: I always said something positive when they left the car. Like "have a nice day," "do well," "have a great day, etc." Well Carlin said something to the effect of, "why do we always say the same boring things when we greet people?" and he suggested some alternatives, like "Have a crappy day!" So the very next day when I dropped my son off to school I said quite loudly as he got out of the car, "Have a crappy day!" His response was, "Dad!...." But he was smiling and it's always best when they start their day off with a smile.

I was smiling, too. So you know how my day started, also.

Since then there have been many variations.

One other example is a "game" I play with my daughter. Just about every time I see her at some point in time I will ask her "How old are you today?" I get the same response from her as my son's response was above, "Dad...!" But it is a game we play and enjoy. I'll probably think of something else eventually.

Have fun with them. Be creative. Have some laughs! You'll be glad you did!

Discipline

This is always a big issue in all families. I won't tell you HOW to discipline (there are thousands of expert opinions you can go to if you want specific ideas), but here are my favorite recommendations.

do it from Love

You've heard the expression, "It hurts me more than it hurts them." If you love your kids, this will be a very true statement. If you love your kids, you will learn to stop and think before you react. Love your kids first!

Being **patient** with children can be tough but it pays off. It shows your love.

stop and think

If you just react to your kids, you will probably be sorry. If you pause, even for one deep breath, your mind will kick in and you will very likely find a better response or reaction. That single breath will give you the opportunity to be creative in your response and to find the best possible way of dealing with the concern.

be firm

It is okay to be firm with your children. You are protecting them from an environment they don't understand and have very limited experience with (in direct contrast to what they sometimes think as teenagers!). You are also, always, educating them. However, remember above all else, that **what you do** and **how you do** it **should come from a basis of love**.

From a psychological standpoint being firm means setting boundaries and sticking to them. One of the most common problems in parenting is setting up some "rules" or boundaries and then not sticking to them. Children may not like the boundaries you set, but if you are consistent in maintaining those guidelines they will know what the limits are.

If you couple this type of loving firmness with good communications with your children (see immediately below this), you will probably have limited discipline problems. One of the sidelights of all of this is that you need to be consistent in what **you** do and say, also. This becomes a learning experience for the parents, too!

listen

Listen to them--really listen! You may be incredibly and pleasantly surprised at their logic (this especially applies to teenagers!). If you listen to them carefully, they will be much more likely to listen to you:

talk to your children

I mean really talk to them. If you have paid attention to them, they will most likely pay attention to you. This has to be a two-way give and take. Children (even teenagers) will listen to your perspective and your logic if you give them a chance to be heard as well. Keep those lines of communications open!

have fun with them!

When is the last time you had fun with your children? I will guarantee that if you spend time with them "on their turf" you will have far fewer discipline problems. This is another way of showing that you care.

be a kid yourself

So often we react from the "adult" in us and unfortunately have forgotten what being a child was like. Spend a moment putting yourself in the child's situation. It may not be such a big problem after all.

Try to remember what it was like to be a kid. Your understanding will go a long way to helping you deal with problems. When you remember your childhood you stand a much better chance of being kind and loving with your children even in difficult circumstances.

Vacations and Weekends

Let's take another brief diversion and discuss another area in which we typically spend a great deal of time with our families or those who are special in our lives. I talked very briefly earlier in the "WORK" section about the importance of taking breaks and taking vacations, but I would like to extend this a bit in relationship to your family.

Vacations

Family vacations can be major events in the life of your loved ones and yourself. You may spend several years gearing up financially and doing the detailed planning for a trip to Florida and Disneyland, or Hawaii, or Europe, or wherever. Probably the most important thing to keep in mind when planning a vacation is to remember what the purpose is: **vacations are to have fun.**

So **vacate** your regular world and have some fun. Leave all that other stuff behind, leave aside all the worries and focus on what is important--sharing time with your family.

Other than that I highly recommend you keep in tune with all the progress you're making on your perfect day "work." Take along your list of guidelines, your by now crumpled notes and keep smiling. Everyone will have a better time!

Weekends

I think the important element about weekends is that they are supposed to be a rest period from work. However you spend the days you have off, you should look to accomplish two main things: have time for yourself away from your work and have time for your family. (Oh! And remember to relax and have fun with both of these!)

This goes especially for us workaholics. If you choose to work on the weekends, if at all possible make your "work" stuff you need to do for the family or yourself and different from your "office" work. Try not to bring all that stuff home from the office. (Did I just hear a "Yeah, but....?")

puttering

I'm a great putterer! As a matter of fact that is probably a great definition for part of my typical weekend--I putter about with this and that. If you have any concept by this time of how my mind works, I tend to move from one puttering thing to another without much rhyme or reason it seems, but most of the time I'm having fun doing the little things that need to be done.

If it feels good, you're probably on the right track.

Your intimate partner

❦

One of the most important relationships in your life is the one you are having with your intimate partner. The success of this relationship is all important to who you are and how you are enjoying your life. The following recommendations expand on many things already said throughout this book. Take the time to perceive how these directly relate to your current relationship. You'll be glad you did.

Affection

Love, affection, caring--we all need it, we all want it, but boy are we sometimes wearing two left shoes when it comes to being able to give or receive it. It seems to be difficult to imagine but many, many couples--who really care for each other--manage to lose the most important means of communicating their love and caring that they have.

How can we keep the affection and love in our relationships?

Show it!

Someone has to take the initiative! If you've moved away in your significant relationship from hugging and holding hands and kissing (except for the "obligatory" peck), then someone has to start the ball rolling. This can be a gradual increase in efforts to bring this back into your relationship, or it can be through actual communication with your partner. You should always be able to ask for what you need and want, and you should always be willing to ask your partner what he/she needs and wants. It might be awkward at first, but it is well worth the effort.

Say it!

This is for **both** men and women. It never ceases to amaze me how many people find it so-o-o-o difficult to express their feelings. And please--both men and women have difficulty with this!!!

The only way to overcome this inability to openly communicate your feelings to your partner is to start. It's really not as difficult as you might think to say something like, "Honey, I want you to know that I really love you."

Try something. Plan ahead. Work up to it. Find the right moment.

Once you do it--the next time is immensely easier. It gets easier each time.

If you have never done this before--Boy will they be pleasantly surprised.

They might even think you're up to something! (You are--loving them!)

Rediscover each other!

Let me give you one example: remember the first time you held hands with someone. Wow! It's amazing how sensual that experience was. One can literally "make love" holding hands. Try revisiting that experience with your partner. If you want to, you can get them involved in the whole process by telling them what you want to do and why. Or you can just surprise them. (This is a "discovery" technique that is used in a wide variety of ways in couples therapy!)

Take their hand and explore it sensually. Remember the wonderful feeling of that first touch...relish the sensations as you explore your partner's hand and as he/she explores yours...pay attention to your senses...focus on the here and now with no regard for anything else but the pleasure you are experiencing and giving. Caress... fondle...play...live a unique moment in time because this moment is as special as the first time...you are a new person today and so is your partner...experience their newness and your own...

Love with your senses again...they have never left you; you just stopped paying attention.

Sex

Explore the possibilities...

Be creative!
Have fun again!

Focus!

Pay attention to your partner!

Ask them what they like--tell them what you like. Sex is a give and take--a special giving and taking. Communicate/listen/know each other.

Sex is the most extreme way you can share yourself with another. Relish that.

Try to understand why they like what they like--their body is different from yours--their experiences are different from yours. If you are both living a caring and loving relationship, then the positive experiences you can have with your partner are literally endless.

Learn from each other--it can be lots of fun and very pleasurable, too.

Explore each other for the first time--again!

Always be loving!

Always be kind!

You might even have to be patient. And that can be fun, too--try it!

Cultivate thy garden--you'll have to explore what that is, won't you?

Two different people

One of the most important things, one of the most wonderful things about life is that we are all unique individuals. It seems so strange to me, then, that we spend so much time trying to change other people--especially our significant other.

I sincerely believe that we are often attracted to people who have many of the opposite characteristics of ourselves. I think this is because the other person really does complement us as a person and I also think it is because there is **so much we can learn from them!**

WoW! Think about that for a minute.

there is another side to life

There are morning people and night people. If you are a morning person that doesn't mean night people are wrong.

There are very romantic (free spirited, liberal) people and very classical (ordered, conservative) people (and everyone in-between). Romantic people--discover the classic side of life with your partner, friends. Classic people-

-find out what all those romantics are so excited about.

Relish the differences in your partner--learn from them--find out what makes them tick differently from you. Try to understand that they view the world differently from you, and that different views are neither right nor wrong but unique. You may find that there are all kinds of things you were missing in life.

If you keep trying to change them to how you view things, you will probably just create a whole bunch of conflicts in your life, in their life, in your lives together. **Discover the joy of discovering "the other side."**

Surprise them!

Almost every couple tries to remember the important days: birthdays, Christmas, anniversaries, etc. Try remembering silly days, or non-days--remember the "Un-birthday" party in **Alice in Wonderland**?

Celebrating your feelings for your partner at "odd" times is a great way to keep your romance fresh and to even keep your partner "on their toes" so to speak.

265

Find unique, small ways to give the special person in your life a "warm fuzzie." This can be a tiny gift, flowers "just because," a phone call, or a small remembrance. Get creative. Be loving.

Give them a foot massage. Who knows what benefits that may produce!

Help them out

I believe that how much one does within the every day business of a relationship is really not as big an issue as getting a break from all of that routine. Give your partner a break every once in a while--I bet they'll help you out, too.

Even if it's not your "job" or your turn, you can quietly help out: take out the trash, do the dishes, mow the lawn, fix that chair, or just offer to help with one of those things you know absolutely nothing about, but your partner may appreciate your help. Who knows, you just might learn something--about the task, about yourself, and about your significant other.

Addendum

So much has already been said in this book about a wide variety of relationships. Revisit these suggestions and apply them specifically to your intimate relationship. Here are a few reminders:

Be willing to talk about it.

Listen to them--really listen!

Be affirming--own your own feelings (blame leads to defensiveness and fights.)

Be kind--always!

Understand that we all make mistakes--practice forgiving

Add some humor to your relationship

Use your head AND your heart.

Open your heart--daily.

Be honest with them--always.*

*Remember that this means you have to be

honest with yourself!

Give them some space.

Crises Management

❧

I have left this until now because if you have read through this book and begun working on some of the suggestions herein; you will have already begun to develop all the "tools" you need for managing the crises in your life. The only difference is in degree.

Crises can take many forms: loss of job, death in the family, severe and terminal illnesses, sudden or difficult problems in the family, accidents, etc. The following recomendations focus on the positive things you can do to help in a crisis situation. Go back to specific discussions in the book to give yourself additional help. I know it is very difficult to do, but this too will pass and you will have changed as a result. Perhaps, just maybe, there is a reason for everything that happens and it is often very difficult to understand at the time.

Think, pray, meditate

Find help in/apply the ***"Eleven Recommendations for a Better Life."***

Be in touch with your **spirituality**.

Be in touch with your **feelings**. It is okay to feel whatever it is you are feeling.

Seek support: intimate partner, spouse, friend, minister, group

Seek help: that's what professionals are trained for--find the one(s) that are best for your needs.

Take time to **recover** (from any type of crisis--You may not think you need it, but these can be very stressing to your system even if the illness or problem, is someone else's.)

Finishing Your Day

❦

"**W**hat a Day This Has Been. What a Rare Mood I'm In." (Sorry, can't supply the music for these lyrics, but I hope you HAVE had a better day. I hope by this time you have realized that the day we have really is in our own hands. Being upbeat and happy isn't something that is dumped on us. Getting that promotion, or raise, winning that race, or buying that large-screen TV isn't going to make you happy either.

You are going to make **you** happy.

You have to start somewhere.

Take some more time for yourself

As mentioned at the beginning of this book, as a prelude to your Perfect Day, you should spend a brief time reviewing and planning for the next day. You probably made a few mistakes this past day; you probably really did work on some things and deserve a pat on the back. Take a small amount of time to review--be kind to yourself.

Take a small amount of time to plan on things you want to work on tomorrow.

Go to Bed with a Smile!

Think of something wonderful, peaceful, and beautiful as you drift off to sleep...

after all tomorrow just might be your Perfect Day.

Recommended Readings

Many of these writers are mentioned in the text. These, and many others, have made an impact on my life. I urge you to expand your own consciousness and knowledge through a continued commitment of personal growth.

Bach, Richard **Illusions**, Delacorte Press, 1977.

Buscaglia, Leo **Love**, Fawcett, 1972.

Carlson, Richard **Don't Sweat the Small Stuff,** Hyperion, 1997.

Chopra, Deepak **Ageless Body, Timeless Mind**, Harmony, 1993.

Chopra, Deepak **Return of the Rishi**, Houghton Mifflin, 1988.

Dyer, Wayne **Your** Erroneous Zones, Funk & Wagnalls, 1976.

Dyer, Wayne **Your Sacred Self**, Harper, 1995.

Dyer, Wayne **Your Life Begins Now**, Hay House, 1995. (Cassette Tapes).

[Author's Note: Dr. Deepak Chopra and Dr. Wayne Dyer has many self-help/motivational tapes available. See your local bookstore.]

Gallwey, W. Timothy **The Inner Game of Tennis**, Bantam Books, 1974.

Heinlein, Robert **Time Enough for Love**, New English Library, 1974.

Hoff, Benjamin **The Tao of Pooh**, Dutton, 1982.

Hoff, Benjamin **The Te of Piglet**, Dutton, 1992.

Lazear, Jonathon **Meditations for Men Who Do Too Much**, Fireside, 1992.

Pirsig, Robert **Zen and the Art of Motorcycle Maintenance**, Bantam Books, 1994.

Rand, Ayn **Atlas Shrugged**, Signett, 1957.

Ray, Sondra **The Only Diet There Is**, Celestial Arts, 1981.

Ray, Sondra **Loving Relationships**, Celestial Arts, 1980.

Redman, Ben Ray, editor **The Portable Voltaire**, Viking, 1949.

Schaef, Anne Wilson **Meditations for Women Who Do Too Much**, Fireside, 1990.

Siegel, Bernie **Peace, Love, and Healing**, Harper & Row, 1989.

Siegel, Bernie **Love, Medicine, and Miracles**, Harper & Row, 1986.

Dr. Joseph E. Koob

Dr. Koob is a dynamic motivational speaker who is available for presentations, workshops and stress/management consulting. His extensive work in the education and counseling fields gives him a unique, practical approach to life and its problems. For further information about presentations and workshops, contact Dr. Koob at NEJS Publications, P.O. Box 3362, Lawton. OK, 73507. Or call 580 357 4538 and leave a message.

Presentations:

"Eleven Recommendations for a Better Life"

"Bringing Love Back Into Your Life"

"How to Have More Fun With Your Life"

"Food for Thought"
(The best diet there is!)
and others

For further information contact:
NEJS Publications
5001 NE Dearborn
Lawton, OK 73507

Final Word

Readers/friends I hope this work proves of some value to you as you move along whatever paths you travel in life. Also, I hope to spend a good part of the rest of my life helping and encouraging others. In that vein I am open to constructive comments and suggestions as I work on a new book, "A Perfect Day for Teenagers." (See address next page.) Since I have one teenager in my house and another one moving along toward that age more rapidly than I would like to think, it is probably appropriate timing.

A final word from a poem by J.R.R. Tolkien, that I feel epitomizes life. Be eager for the new day! Be eager for your new paths!

"The Road goes ever on and on
    Down from the door where it began.
Now far ahead the Road has gone,
    And I must follow, if I can,
Pursuing it with eager feet,
    Until it joins some larger way,
Where many paths and errands meet.
    and whither then? I cannot say."*

*J.R.R. Tolkien, **The Fellowship of the Ring**, Ballantine, 1965.

Ordering Information:

If you would like an **autographed** copy of "*A Perfect Day*" contact the address below and send a check or money order. Include the following information:

Please indicate if you would like a brief message included:

_____

Number of copies: _____ @ $8.50   _____(total)

       Postage and handling   _____

       1 copy: $3.50
       2 copies: $4.50
       3 copies: $5.50
       4 or more: $6.50

       Total enclosed: _____

NEJS PUBLICATIONS
P.O. Box 3362
Lawton, OK 73507